Creative Dance

Enriching Understanding

Sheryle Bergmann Drewe

Detselig Enterprises Ltd.

Calgary, Alberta, Canada

Canadian Cataloguing in Publication Data

Drewe, Sheryle Bergmann, 1964-

    Creative dance

ISBN 1-55059-130-4

    1. Dance—Study and teaching.   2. Dance for children.
I. Title.

GV1589.D73 1996   372.6′6   C96-910153-8

Detselig Enterprises Ltd.
210-1220 Kensington Rd. N.W.
Calgary, Alberta T2N 3P5

Detselig Enterprises Ltd. appreciates the financial support for our 1996 publishing program provided by the Department of Canadian Heritage and the Alberta Foundation for the Arts, a beneficiary of the Lottery Fund of the Government of Alberta.

Printed in Canada   ISBN 1-55059-130-4   SAN 115-0324

To Joshua

whose imaginative outlook has been a constant
source of inspiration.

Table of Contents

Acknowledgements

I would like to take this opportunity to thank all who have helped me in the realization of this book. *Creative Dance* is derived from my doctoral thesis and special thanks are due to the members of my examining committee: Dr. Sharon Bailin, Dr. Romulo Magsino, Dr. Neil Winther, Dr. Ian Winchester, and Dr. Murdith McLean. I would like to devote an extra special thanks to my advisor, Dr. Sharon Bailin. Not only did she provide detailed feedback on my work, she has proven to be a constant role model and mentor. She has made the "academic world" an inviting and exciting place for me.

Thanks are also due to Dr. Henry Janzen and Ms. Joyce Fromson. Their support and encouragement for my professional development is something for which I will always be grateful.

I must also thank my family and friends who have been a constant source of support and understanding. Without such support, it would have been impossible to spend the time needed to complete such a task. Finally, I want to thank my son Joshua, who has demonstrated incredible patience with "mommy and her papers." My hope is that all of those evenings of thesis work interspersed with "puppet play breaks" will have left him with a taste for the pleasure which can be derived from academic pursuits.

I would like to acknowledge the assistance of a doctoral fellowship from the Social Sciences and Humanities Research Council of Canada.

This book is based, in part, on some of my earlier writings and I would like to thank the publishers for permission to use parts of the following articles: "An Objective Aesthetics? Implications for Arts Education," *Paideusis* 8,1 (1994); "An Epistemological Justification for Aesthetic Experience," *The Journal of Aesthetic Education* 27,2 (1993); "Creative Dance in the Education Curriculum: Justifying the Unambiguous," *Canadian Journal of Education* 20,2 (1995); "The Creative Imagination or the Imaginative Creation: Implications for Creative Dance Education," *Avante* 1,2 (1995); "Imagining the Imaginative: An Analysis and Implications for Arts Education," *Interchange* (forthcoming, 1997); "A Justification for the Inclusion of the Arts in Education," *The Journal of Educational Thought*, 1995 Philosophy of Education Society Proceedings.

This book has been published with the help of a grant from the Social Science Federation of Canada, using funds provided by the Social Sciences and Humanities Research Council of Canada.

Preface

The purpose of this book is to provide a clear, coherent justification for the inclusion of creative dance in the educational curriculum; to show why creative dance should be included in the curriculum and what creative dance education would have to look like in order to provide this sort of educational value. The justification I propose for the inclusion of creative dance is based on its potential to foster a rich understanding of the human experience. If one is to foster understanding through creative dance, then creative dance education must involve the appreciation and creation of works with aesthetic features.

In chapter one, I suggest that creative dance's strongest educational value lies within its aesthetic nature. Chapter two involves an examination of what is meant by an aesthetic nature. In chapter three, I provide a justification for creative dance by arguing that its aesthetic nature makes it possible for participants in creative dance activities to attain a unique understanding of the human experience. What form creative dance education has to take to provide this knowledge is the focus of chapter four, where I consider what it means to create and appreciate works with aesthetic features. I contrast the approach of creating and appreciating works with aesthetic features and prevalent approaches to fostering creativity in dance education (and education in general). Contrary to the belief that creativity is fostered primarily through "free expression" activities, I argue that creativity involves the creation of original works with aesthetic features. Much of the confusion regarding the idea of creativity in dance education is a result of conflating the imaginative with the creative. Thus, in chapter five I examine what is meant by imaginative activities, and not only how these differ from creative activities, but how imaginative activities are still necessary for creating works which foster understanding. Finally, I consider in chapter six the practical implications of a justification based on the understanding gained through aesthetic experience, and the form which creative dance education has to take as a result of this justification.

Chapter I

Creative Dance in the Curriculum

Creative dance in the educational curriculum has been non-existent at worst and peripheral at best. Most people do not consider creative dance to be a "real subject", unlike mathematics or language arts. Rather, it has a status similar to that of drama. Just as many school systems consider drama to be a part of the language arts program, creative dance is usually considered a part, albeit a small one, of the physical education curriculum. Unlike drama, creative dance is not usually viewed as an activity to be offered as extra-curricular; that is, drama clubs are much more prominent than creative dance clubs. Why is creative dance so often limited to a peripheral position in the physical education class? Why does it not share the same status as mathematics and language arts? A reason implied by proponents of the "back to the basics" movement (of which, needless to say, creative dance is not a part) is the lack of cognitive content in activities such as creative dance. However, creative dance *does* have cognitive content. In fact, the most convincing justification for the inclusion of creative dance in the educational curriculum is its potential to foster understanding of the human experience.

Many scholars have attempted to justify a position for dance in the curriculum. The literature concerning creative dance contains some rather grandiose claims.

Creative dance refers to bodily activities that express inner thoughts and feelings and enhance those thoughts and feelings. This art form emphasizes creativity, problem solving, and the expression of thoughts and feelings.[1]

Creative movement represents a specialized art form with tremendous educational potential for children. It amalgamates the physical, affective, and intellectual components of the child. It stimulates and enriches the creative personality and plants a promise for imagination and achievement which may easily extend beyond today's visions.[2]

Dance in the educational environment is more than a physical phenomenon. The participant learns to be intellectually curious, to engage in critical thinking and to be intimately involved in problem solving, which generates imaginative, inventive, and expressive responses.[3]

Creative dance provides alternative and supplemental avenues to instruction. It is not a frill or an afterthought, but an integral part of learning, a way of opening all areas of learning and of stimulating the educational process.[4]

The arts and especially creative dance are basic to a child's education because they foster the development of a positive self-concept. The central part of self-concept is the bodily self; and creative experience with bodily self is fundamental to education, to development, to self-fulfillment, and ultimately to society.[5]

There is a certain vagueness to many of the claims made. For example, MacDonald offers the claim that "creative dance emphasizes problem-solving," without suggestion as to how this takes place. For the claim that creative dance "plants a promise for imagination," Wells does not explicate the concept of imagination. With respect to the claim that "it stimulates the educational process," Blackwell does not indicate what is meant by the educational process. There are also some potential contradictions. For example, if creative dance is viewed as a means to learning other subject areas or as a means to developing a positive self-concept, should it be called an art form? We typically consider art to be intrinsically rather than instrumentally valuable. Although art may be valuable for its own sake, does this negate its potential as a means to other ends? At what point would creative dance move from the realm of art to the realm of therapy? Are these emphases dichotomous? Not only is it important to clarify the claims made for creative dance, it is also important to examine the arguments offered in support of them. Many scholars simply state their claims with no supporting arguments. Others offer seriously flawed arguments. I intend to justify the inclusion of creative dance in the educational curriculum and to provide supporting arguments for this claim.

Dance Forms

In order to provide a justification for creative dance, we must first determine what creative dance is. I will consider the place of creative dance in the realm of dance forms. I will also discuss the main views regarding creative dance, as well as what is acceptable and what is problematic with each of these views.

The common element found in all forms of dance is the rhythmical movement of the body for aesthetic purposes, but how this is achieved varies. If you were to view dance forms (e.g., ballet, jazz, tap) on a continuum, you would typically place creative dance at one end with ballet at the opposite end. Ballet is one of the most structured forms of dance, with little leeway for personal expression on the part of the dancers. Creative dance, on the other hand, typically involves a large degree of "self-expression." Ballet movements have a long history and there is a correct way to perform each movement. Although the director of a ballet may take license in varying the number of dancers on stage, entries and exits, costumes, set design, etc., he/she cannot change how, for example, an arabesque is supposed to look. In creating new ballets, the choreographer has the freedom to juxtapose certain movements, but the ballet tradition governs how these movements are to be performed. As for the dancers, they have no freedom to change a ballet movement and there is usually little opportunity for them to choreograph movements in a dance piece. In other words, ballet dancers must conform to the tradition of ballet as well as to directions from the choreographer or director.

Jazz and tap dance are similar to ballet in that particular movements and techniques have been developed as part of these traditions. However, dancers usually have more leeway in jazz and tap than in ballet to incorporate some improvised movements. Jazz or tap choreographers will sometimes choreograph a dance in such a way that a portion of the dance piece is devoted to improvised movement on the part of the dancers. So, although certain jazz steps and tap technique are learned, there is the potential for dancers to incorporate some of their own movements.

Folk and social dance are similar to jazz and tap in that certain steps and sequences have developed over time. However, participants usually have a large degree of freedom in these forms to "add their own touch." What is meant by "their own" in regard to folk dance needs some clarification. Folk dance results from dances developed among the common "folk." The common folk are constituents of particular cultures, and thus, folk dances are culturally specific. Hence, dancers will adapt a step common to many cultures (e.g., the *schottische*) to fit the dances of their particular culture. Regarding social dance, participants' "own touch" will be more personal. When people waltz or fox trot, they perform certain steps, but how they arrange them and how they dance with a partner will be more of a personal expression than, for instance, a *pas de deux* in ballet.

Modern dance is probably closest to the creative dance end of the continuum in that there is a lot of room, especially for the choreographer, to create movements for a dance piece.

Like jazz and tap, dancers often have an opportunity within the dance piece to improvise movements. As well, modern dance is more like theatre than ballet in that the dancers are given an opportunity to add their own "personal touch" to the piece. The dancer and the choreographer often are one and the same person in modern dance. Because of the opportunity to improvise and choreograph, modern dance is most similar to creative dance. In fact, we may perceive modern dance as an advanced form of creative dance, just as we view artistic gymnastics as the follow up to educational gymnastics. However, there is an important difference between modern dance and creative dance. Modern dance does not have a very long history, but since its inception, certain movements have been adopted and modified from other dance forms. These movements have become part of a modern dancer's repertoire. Thus, modern dance is becoming, to a limited degree, like ballet in that years of training in technique are required. Although creative dance involves skill in using movement elements, years of training in technique are not required before participants are able to choreograph dance pieces.

Before going into more detail regarding what creative dance involves, I must make one further distinction between creative dance and other dance forms. I have suggested that the criteria common to all dance forms is the movement of the body for aesthetic purposes, but some might object that another criterion should be the relationship of this movement to music. However, although music is intimately connected to the dance forms of ballet, jazz, tap, folk and social dance, this is not the case with modern and creative dance. In fact, modern dance developed in part as a reaction against traditional forms of dance. Along with the rejection of formalized movements, modern dancers rejected the necessity of music for movement to be called dance. Although rhythm is still a component of modern dance, dancers experience rhythm not only through music, but also percussion, body sounds, poetry, literature and the visual arts. The use of other art forms as stimuli for movement is also evident in the teaching of creative dance. So although music is often a stimulus for creative dance, it is not a necessary component and thus the existence of music with movement is not a criterion common to all dance forms.

The preceding discussion may give the impression that the only difference between the various dance forms is the degree of structure involved and the use or non-use of music as a stimulus. Although there are differences in style and nature of movements particular to each dance form, it is beyond the scope of this book to go into a detailed description of these. However, I should make one further point concerning the purpose of different dance forms. Sparshott makes a useful distinction when he distinguishes between three kinds of dances.

> *There are ethnic dances, danced as part of a way of life in which they play a structural or ideological role; there are social dances, which groups of people dance together just as a means of endorsing their togetherness; and there are art dances, which are danced in studios and theatres and belong to the same world as concert halls and art galleries.*[6]

Folk dance would fall under the ethnic dances category, social dance would fall under the social dances category, and ballet, tap, jazz, modern and creative dance would fall under the art dances category. Most scholars would consider none of these categorizations contentious, except perhaps the placment of creative dance in the art dances category. However, this is exactly where creative dance should be placed. Before detailing this argument, it is important to clarify what I mean by creative dance.

What is Creative Dance?

I must make a distinction between "creative dance" and "creative" dance. In chapter four, I will discuss the criteria necessary for labelling something as creative and suggest that if any dance form meets these criteria, one could label it "creative". "Creative dance," on the other hand, is a particular form of dance. Elementary school teachers teach creative dance because it does not require the years of training demanded by other dance forms. Basically, creative dance involves the use of movement elements to express thoughts and feelings. Creative dance has been defined by many dance practitioners and theoreticians as an expression of the inner self through the medium of movement.[7] Dimondstein expands upon this definition as "the interpretation of a child's ideas, feelings, and sensory impressions expressed symbolically in movement forms through the unique use of his body."[8] Creative dance teachers may suggest particular ideas or feelings which they want their students to express through movement. Teachers could also provide a stimulus, e.g., a piece of music, a poem, a painting, for students to interpret and express through the medium of movement.

We can further define the medium of movement using the elements of movement. Rudolf Laban carried out a comprehensive analysis of movement and categorized movement into its constituent elements. Examples of Laban's movement elements include body awareness; space awareness; the awareness of weight, time and flow; and the adaptation to partners and groups.[9] The movement themes developed from these elements have formed the basis of numerous handbooks on creative dance.[10] Although Morin has criticized the curriculum content proposed by these writers as too myopic,[11] we should view the development of an elemental movement vocabulary as having a wider purpose, that being to express the inner self. In fact, Joyce states that the goal of creative dance is "to communicate through movement"[12] and Preston-Dunlop's handbook includes a theme which she refers to as "Meaning, Expression, Communication and Embodiment."[13] Creative dance, then, is not simply what Morin refers to as "elemental dance" (dance whose content is based solely upon the utilization of movement elements) but it also includes aspects of what she refers to as "expressive dance" (dance dealing with the aesthetic qualities and qualitative relationships).[14] Whether the focus is on the elemental or expressive aspects of creative dance is often a function of who is viewing the activity.

Different sectors of the educational system view creative dance differently. Some sectors consider creative dance to be part of the physical education curriculum. Others have considered placing dance under the rubric of arts education. The aspect of creative dance emphasized reflects the position to which educators relegate creative dance in the curriculum. As part of the physical education curriculum, the focus of creative dance lessons is on the development of motor skills, with little emphasis on the aesthetic potential of the experience. In the realm of arts education, the aesthetic potential of creative dance is the primary focus. Besides an emphasis on motor skills or aesthetic potential, educators have viewed creative dance as a means to improve students' self-concepts and as a means to learn other subject areas. I will examine the views of creative dance as physical education, as therapy, as integration and as art, as well as indicate what is acceptable and what is problematic with each of these views.

Dance as Physical Education

Movement is not dance, but all dance involves movement.[15]

A focus on the movement involved in creative dance has resulted in its inclusion in the physical education curriculum in some school systems. However, one can view movement in more than one way. Stanley makes a distinction between functional and expressive movement.

> *Functional or objective movement and subjective or expressive movement offer the participant two opposing experiences. Objective movement may be defined as the type which is geared to accomplish a practical task. Simple examples are to kick a ball; to vault over a fence; to pull a sled . . .*

> *Expressive movement conveys a thought or feeling. The body is the instrument of communication. Simple examples of expressive movements are: the angry stamp of a foot; a startled jump of fright; a slow, cautious tiptoeing. The interpretation of expressive actions is not as simple a matter as that of understanding or assessing objective movement.*[16]

We typically view dance as employing expressive movement, while we consider most sports skills to be functional in nature. However, this dichotomy is not so obvious when one considers what Best refers to as 'aesthetic' sports:

> *there is a category of sports in which the aim cannot be specified in isolation from the aesthetic, for example, synchronized swimming, trampolining, gymnastics, figure-skating and diving. I shall call these 'aesthetic' sports since they are similar to the arts in that their purpose cannot be considered apart from the manner of achieving it. . . . For instance, it would make no sense to suggest to a figure-skater that it did not matter how he performed his movements, as long as he achieved the purpose of the sport, since that purpose inevitably concerns the manner of performance.*[17]

Although aesthetic sports appear to involve only expressive movement, the functional nature of movement is also present. One of the objectives of involvement in an aesthetic sport is to gain dominance over a competitor. Krohn notes this point.

> *But sport is not dance, and dance is not sport. The objective of the two activities is different. In sport, the objective is to win the game or gain dominance over a competitor, and the opportunity to gain dominance over the opponent depends on the skill level. In dance, however, the goal is to communicate an idea or feeling, and therefore, the stress is on the quality of the movement, in order to make it more meaningful.*[18]

Krohn's comment ushers in another area in need of elucidation, that of skill acquisition. Dimondstein suggests that "dance is geared neither toward the refinement of skills in themselves nor toward competitive ends. Skills become the means by which each individual grapples with the elements of dance to shape a personal statement."[19] This distinct purpose of acquiring skills for dance has led Carr to scrutinize the emphasis placed on "behavioral objectives" by many physical educationalists. Carr argues *that a behavioral objectives approach to the teaching of physical and practical pursuits in general, and to the activity of dance in particular, is cripplingly limited to the extent that it is dominated or constrained by a particular view of theoretical psychology that persists in an attempt to understand skill learning in terms of conditioning and reinforcement, associations between stimuli and responses or some elaboration of these notions in the guise of a "psychomotor" model of skill acquisition.*[20]

Although the "psychomotor" model of skill acquisition dominates the teaching of physical education, Carr notes that there is a significant problem in applying such a model to the teaching of creative dance. Creative dance skills are not the same as sports skills in their ability to be conditioned. Carr suggests that a necessary condition of creativity is a certain degree of autonomy involved in creative conduct. He emphasizes that by autonomy, he does not mean unconstrained freedom. In fact, he advocates the necessity of teaching dance skills and knowledge. However, he points out that by teaching skills and knowledge, one cannot necessarily predetermine the outcome of their application.

To state that creative conduct cannot be conditioned, then, is to express a conceptual point rather than merely to comment on the limits of technical possibility. If it is creative or expressive dance that we are interested in, then, the job of the teacher is to acquaint pupils with dance skills and techniques, knowledge of dance-artistic conventions, and traditional forms and to equip them with a repertoire of abilities to perform particular movements, but always with a view to their being able eventually to act autonomously in the light of this knowledge, understanding, and skill.[21]

A more detailed discussion of conditions for creativity will be the focus of chapter four. At this point, it is sufficient to note that if the outcome of creative conduct requires some degree of autonomy, the teaching of the skills involved will not necessarily fit the "psychomotor" model of skill acquisition. Since this is the predominant model of physical education classes, the outcome of this argument necessitates either moving creative dance out of the realm of physical education or expanding our conception of physical education to include other models of skill acquisition.

Since physical skills are a necessary component of creative dance, there is nothing wrong with including it in the physical education curriculum. However, not only do models of skill acquisition have to accommodate the conditions for creative conduct, teachers of creative dance have to be aware of the potential for aesthetic experience in dance. If creative dance involved nothing more than the development of physical skills, one would be hard pressed to justify the inclusion of dance over other activities whose focus is also on the development of motor skills. A prime example of such an activity is educational gymnastics. Although educational gymnastics activities may involve creating routines, the purpose of such routines is primarily to display an understanding of motor skills as opposed to the expression of thoughts or feelings. If creative dance did not offer anything beyond what is offered by educational gymnastics, there would be no reason (other than variety) to include creative dance in the curriculum.

Dance theoreticians have suggested that creative dance does offer something not offered by activities such as educational gymnastics: the potential for an aesthetic experience. McColl suggests that "what distinguishes the content of children's dance from movement education [educational gymnastics] is its specific emphasis on the expressive and the aesthetic."[22] A realization of this aesthetic potential has implications for the physical education teacher.

Dance at the physical education level has often been taught as a series of movement skills with little thought given to its aesthetic and artistic side. No time has been given to areas such as history or dance appreciation, which are a very important part of dance education. Ensuring that physical educators who are going out to teach have some background in these areas is of the utmost importance.[23]

Krohn's suggestion that to realize the aesthetic/artistic side of dance requires some background on the part of the teacher is a point well taken. Physical education teachers cannot realize the potential of the aesthetic nature of creative dance without taking some necessary steps in that direction. In conclusion, the recognition of the aesthetic potential of creative dance is an essential element in teaching this activity. Thus, dance can be viewed as a part of physical education, but an expansion of the conception of physical education to include the aesthetic is necessary.

Dance as Therapy

The expressive nature of creative dance entails an expansion of the concept of physical education to include the aesthetic. The expressive nature of creative dance has also resulted in many dance practitioners and theoreticians espousing the therapeutic potential of creative dance. The therapeutic potential of dance becomes obvious when dance theoreticians advocate creative dance as a means to help children develop positive self-concepts and self-acceptance. Murray expresses this sentiment when she credits creative dance with providing

> *a primary medium for expression involving the total self (not just a part, like the voice) or totally separated from the physical self (like painting or sculpture). Dance and the movement that produces it is 'me' and, as such, is the most intimate of expressive media. A child's self-concept, his own identity and self-esteem are improved in relation to such use of his body's movement.*[24]

Alter reiterates the emphasis on the "me" or the personal nature of creative dance when she states that "during a creative dance experience, children engage in problem-finding activity in which their own bodies provide the means of solution. This can enhance children's sense of bodily self and contribute to a positive self-concept."[25]

Justifying the inclusion of creative dance in the educational curriculum on the basis of its therapeutic value raises the question of whether education is the same as therapy. If they are not the same, how does a different emphasis affect the teaching of creative dance and what *should* be the emphasis in an educational setting?

The aims of the teacher and therapist are different. Arnold emphasizes this contention.

> *The aims and objectives of the teacher are not those of the therapist. Although therapeutic effects may stem from the work of the teacher of aesthetic or expressive activities, these are not the reason for their being taught. The teacher as educator is concerned with introducing the pupil to these activities for their own inherent values rather than for other benefits which may fortuitously accrue as a result of engaging in them. The educator and the therapist have different purposes, even though the outcomes of their efforts may in fact to some extent overlap.*[26]

If one is teaching creative dance as an expressive activity having aesthetic value, one should realize that its therapeutic benefits are side-effects, not the main purpose of the activity. Therapeutic and educational benefits are often conflated, especially by those who view education as involving personal growth. However, if the aim of education is personal growth, we must raise the question of how a teacher would know if growth was occurring. The teacher could only know if growth occurred through some form of assessment. As Best points out, "a teacher needs to know whether, and to what extent, his students are understanding and learning, and to achieve such knowledge is assessment. To fail to assess is to fail to teach."[27] To push the argument further, if the teacher realizes that the child is not growing, he/she must intervene. As Best puts it, "to refuse to intervene is to refuse to educate."[28] Thus, even if we view education as involving personal growth, we must do something to ensure that growth is occurring (assessment) and if growth is not occurring, we must do something to change this (intervention). This is not necessarily what happens in a therapeutic setting. In a therapeutic setting, growth has ceased for some reason. The aim of the therapist, then, is to find the cause of this cessation of growth; e.g., some particular experience. Therapists have used creative dance with emotionally disturbed people as a way of expressing particular experiences which they are unable to recount verbally. If an individual engages in creative dance within a therapeutic setting as opposed to an educational one, how the activity is taught will differ. This difference has important implications for the justification of creative dance in an *educational* curriculum.

When a person experiences dance as therapy, artistic form takes a back seat to the content of what is being expressed, e.g., a particular experience. Dimondstein differentiates between "self-expression," which she defines as giving *vent* to feelings that may be random or uncontrolled and reflect the way a person feels at the moment, and "artistic expression," which is giving *form* to feelings that are either evoked or controlled in relation to the sensuous qualities of a medium, the organization of materials and response to the subject.[29] In a therapeutic setting, where people are physically expressing experiences which they have not been able to vocalize, the movement involves "venting" as opposed to "giving form" to feelings; i.e., the content being expressed supersedes the form of the expression. There is value in this sort of expression, but it belongs in a therapeutic, not an educational setting.

As part of an educational curriculum, creative dance involves helping students learn how to give form to their thoughts and feelings through movement. This emphasis on form is important if the teacher is to assess the growth of the students in their ability to express their thoughts and feelings. In chapter two, I will discuss the aesthetic features which give form to such expressions, but at this time it is sufficient to note that these features act as standards for assessment. They are also important as points of focus if the teacher must intervene in an attempt to help students grow in their ability to express their thoughts and feelings. As Bailin suggests, "if expression must necessarily be in a medium, then control of the medium is a prerequisite for expression."[30] To reach this point, students must develop the knowledge of, and become skilled in using, the basic movement elements as well as aesthetic features. Arnold points out that "what is not always appreciated by some child-centered 'free expressionists' is that freedom for creativity and self-expression is not restricted by technical competency but actually enhanced by it."[31] When the necessity of teaching knowledge and skills regarding movement elements and aesthetic features is recognized, the creative dance experience can actually be an educational experience. If creative dance is simply "free expression," children can "do as they please" and there is no need to "educate."

If we view "free expression" experiences as therapeutic, then in advocating the teaching of skills and knowledge in creative dance, we may appear to be denying the potential for therapeutic benefits. Although I have made a distinction between education and therapy, I must reiterate the potential for therapeutic side-effects in the educational setting. If creative dance is expressive in nature, it would seem it would best fulfill its purpose if an audience received the expression. Lockhart and Pease make this connection when they suggest that "a performance is the logical outcome of the dance experience. Without it the ultimate purpose, its communication, cannot be realized."[32] Realizing an attempt at communication can be a satisfying experience for the dancers. "In performing they are experiencing the intent of dance, completing the circuit for the communication of idea that is channeled from purposeful movement to the eye of the beholder."[33] This communication with others has the potential for developing self-concept. The development of self-concept results when an audience approves of the communication which it experiences. A performance challenges students to do their best both for their own growth and in order to earn the approval of the audience. Although the opportunity to improve self-concept through the acceptance of one's expression may not be the prime aim of creative dance in an educational setting, we should see it as an important benefit which should be available to students.

Dance as Integration

When we view creative dance as therapy, creative dance becomes a means to building self-esteem, etc. When we view creative dance as a component of an integrated curriculum, it becomes a means to learning other subject areas. MacDonald suggests such an integration.

> *In a curriculum espousing holism, creativity would be of paramount importance in all subjects, the arts would be integrated into all core subjects, and creative dance would have an integral place in the curriculum. For example, mathematical fractions might be taught by rhythmic chanting and movement, poems interpreted through creative dance, or the meaning of the planets, and their positions in the universe instilled by creating dances.[34]*

Other dance practitioners reiterate MacDonald's suggestions. Schul-Pfeffer states that

> *exploring an idea by capitalizing on the child's muscular movement and body position will help him physically recall the idea. For example, a fifth grade child had difficulty understanding the abstractions of "symmetry" and "asymmetry." The idea quickly crystallized for him, however, after he and four other children created a symmetric group shape and then moved into an asymmetric shape.[35]*

Shapiro suggests that

> *once you begin to think of movement as a means of perception, its value as a teaching tool becomes clear. In an algebra class a dancer helped conduct studies in time rates – the children did crabwalks and cartwheels across the room, and others timed and compared them. Elements of physics – gravity, action and reaction, the fulcrum – can be demonstrated vividly with movement.[36]*

Using dance/movement to teach the position of planets, or the concepts of symmetry and gravity, may enhance the teaching of the lesson. However, one should hesitate to denote such an activity as art. If we are to consider creative dance an art form, it must share features characteristic of other art forms, i.e., having a capacity to induce aesthetic satisfaction.[37] Such an end may not result if we use creative dance to teach mathematics, for example.

Another issue which bears upon this discussion concerns the intrinsic value of art. We typically conceive of art as having intrinsic value. Richmond defines the aesthetic "in its most widely accepted sense as a special kind of perceptual attitude or outlook that involves the apprehension of an object, natural or man-made *for its own sake*" [italics added].[38] The apprehension of an object (or performance) for its own sake is clearly not a factor in MacDonald's definition of art. Rather, teachers use art as a means to teach fractions or the positions of the planets. A more detailed discussion of the intrinsic versus the extrinsic value of aesthetic experience will be the focus of chapter three. At this point it is sufficient to note that we need to clarify the purpose of creative dance. I am not denying the value of integrating subject areas. However, we should be concerned when dance is seen as a means to other ends rather than as an end in itself.

A final issue regarding dance as an integratable subject concerns its relation to other subjects. Dimondstein makes an important point when she notes that

> *arbitrary attempts have been made to relate dance to other disciplines without considering organic connections between them in terms of content and methodology — that is, between what is to be learned and the means by which it is best communicated. Certain questions are raised, for example, when dance is related to math through the use of body shapes that are supposed to facilitate the understanding of a number. Is the focus on learning a quantitative symbol system of defined shapes and relationships or on a qualitative kinesthetic process of exploring body parts to symbolize numerical shapes? Furthermore, is such a learning experience designed to humanize math concepts, or is a conception of math intended to enhance the understanding of dance?*[39]

We should give serious consideration to Dimondstein's questions regarding the purpose of integrating subject areas, i.e., is it to humanize mathematics concepts or to enhance the understanding of dance? Too often the zest to integrate subject areas results in a forced relationship. I am not denying the potential for a worthwhile integration of subject areas. However, we need to be cautious in our selection of content from other subject areas if we want to do justice to the concept of creative dance. Dimondstein makes this point when she states that

> *meaning in dance lies in expressive movement and in movement that reflects intellectual content drawn from other disciplines. Ideas must be carefully selected, however. A bridge is needed between dance and subject matter that reflects concepts relevant to students' emotional experiences. The connection must be created through an approach in which subject matter is not "known about" but experienced in a metaphoric relationship — that is, where subject matter becomes a metaphor for human experience. Results are achieved by searching out ways of expressing the subject's dynamic components through the forms of dance.*[40]

Although Dimondstein advocates caution in the attempt to integrate different subject areas, within the arts, there is more leeway for worthwhile integration which does justice to the dance experience as well as to the other art forms. We can justify advocating the integration of various art forms based on the interrelatedness of the arts. This interrelatedness is based on the common aesthetic features which different art forms share. An illumination of the aesthetic features evident in creative dance as well as in other art forms suggests that we should view creative dance as an artistic activity.

A Justification for Dance as Art

Thus far I have discussed creative dance as physical education, as a therapeutic activity, and as a tool for learning other subject areas. Although creative dance may have the benefits of developing motor skills, improving self-concept and enhancing the learning of other subjects, its primary focus should be as an art form. In examining the view of creative dance as physical education, I proposed the need to accommodate "creative" skill acquisition as well as the potential for an "aesthetic" experience. In examining the view of creative dance as therapy, I suggested that we should make a distinction between "self-expression" and "artistic expression," if creative dance is to take place in an *educational* context. In examining the view of creative dance as a tool for integration, I advocated caution so as not to create forced relationships between subject areas and suggested that creative dance seemed to "fit" most easily with other artistic subjects as a result of shared aesthetic features. These conclusions would suggest that the value of creative dance as an art form transcends the values of creative dance as physical education, as therapy and as an integrative tool. I am not denying that creative dance has these other values. I am suggesting that if we want to justify the inclusion of creative dance in the curriculum, we must advocate its strongest value. Since I am suggesting that the strongest value of creative dance lies in its potential as an art form, the following chapter will involve a discussion of what I mean by the aesthetic nature of creative dance.

Notes

1 C. MacDonald, "Creative Dance in Elementary Schools: A Theoretical and Practical Justification," *Canadian Journal of Education* 16 (1991): 434.

2 L. Wells, "Children on the Move," *Design* 80 (Sept. 1979): 18.

3 A. Zirulnik & J. Young, "Help Them 'Jump for Joy'," *Journal of Physical Education and Recreation* 50 (Sept. 1979): 43.

4 C. Blackwell, "Providing Every Child Opportunity to Dance," *Journal of Physical Education and Recreation* 50 (Sept. 1979): 55.

5 J. Alter, "A Manifesto for Creative Dance in the Schools: Arts and Bodies are Basic," *Design* 85 (July/Aug. 1984): 28.

6 F. Sparshott, "Contexts of Dance," *Journal of Aesthetic Education* 24 (Spring, 1990): 79.

7 For example, M. Joyce, *First Steps in Teaching Creative Dance to Children*, 2nd edition (Palo Alto, CA: Mayfield Publishing Company, 1980), p. 1; R. Murray, "A Statement of Belief," in G. Fleming, ed., *Children's Dance* (Washington, D.C.: AAHPER Publications, 1973), p. 5; M. H'Doubler, *Dance: A Creative Art Experience* (Madison, Wisconsin: The University of Wisconsin Press, 1957), p. xxv.

8 G. Dimondstein, *Exploring the Arts with Children* (New York: MacMillan Publishing Co., 1974), p. 167.

9 R. Laban, *Modern Educational Dance*, 3rd edition (Boston: Play, Inc., 1975), pp. 25-51.

10 For example, V. Preston-Dunlop, *A Handbook for Dance in Education* (Estover, Plymouth: MacDonald & Evans Ltd., 1980); Joyce, *First Steps in Teaching Creative Dance to Children*, 2nd ed. (Palo Alto, CA: Mayfield Publishing Company, 1980); J. Boorman, *Creative Dance in the First Three Grades* (Don Mills, Ontario: Longmans Canada, 1969).

11 F. Morin, *Psychological and Curricular Foundations for Elementary Dance Education* (Edina, MN: Bellwether Press, 1988), pp. 66-67.

12 Joyce, *First Steps in Teaching Creative Dance to Children*, p. 1.

13 Preston-Dunlop, *A Handbook for Dance in Education*, p. 168.

14 Morin, *Psychological and Curricular Foundations for Elementary Dance Education*, p. 70.

15 G. Fleming, *Creative Rhythmic Movement: Boys and Girls Dancing* (New Jersey: Prentice-Hall, Inc., 1976), p. 8.

16 S. Stanley, *Physical Education: A Movement Orientation*, 2nd edition (Toronto: McGraw-Hill Ryerson, 1977), p. 33.

17 D. Best, *Philosophy and Human Movement* (London: George Allen & Unwin, 1978), pp. 104-105.

18 J. Krohn, "The Dance Dilemma: Where Does it Fit – Physical Education or Arts Education?" *Canadian Association of Health, Physical Education and Recreation Journal* 57 (Fall 1991): 48.

19 G. Dimondstein, "The Place of Dance in General Education," *Journal of Aesthetic Education* 19 (1985): 81.

[20] D. Carr, "Dance Education, Skill, and Behavioral Objectives," *Journal of Aesthetic Education* 18 (1984): 68.

[21] Ibid., p. 73.

[22] S. McColl, "Dance as Aesthetic Education," *Journal of Physical Education, Health and Recreation* 50 (Sept. 1979): 44.

[23] Krohn, "The Dance Dilemma," p. 49.

[24] Murray, "A Statement of Belief," p. 5.

[25] Alter, "A Manifesto for Creative Dance in the Schools," p. 28.

[26] P. Arnold, "Creativity, Self-Expression, and Dance," *Journal of Aesthetic Education* 20 (1986): 53.

[27] D. Best, *The Rationality of Feeling* (London: Falmer Press, 1992), p. 75.

[28] Ibid., p. 76.

[29] Dimondstein, *Exploring the Arts with Children*, p. 167.

[30] S. Bailin, "Theatre, Drama Education and the Role of the Aesthetic," *Journal of Curriculum Studies* 25 (Sept./Oct. 1993): 428.

[31] Arnold, "Creativity, Self-Expression, and Dance," pp. 54-55.

[32] A. Lockhart & E. Pease, *Modern Dance: Building and Teaching Lessons*, 6th edition (Dubuque, Iowa: W.C. Brown Company Publishers, 1982), p. 28.

[33] Ibid., p. 177.

[34] MacDonald, "Creative Dance in Elementary Schools," p. 436.

[35] J. Schul-Pfeffer, "Creative Dance/Movement as a Teaching Tool," *Design* 82 (Oct. 1980): 35.

[36] L. Shapiro, "Dancing in the Schools," *Design* 79 (Sept. 1978): 10.

[37] H. Meynell, *The Nature of Aesthetic Value* (Albany: State University of New York Press, 1986), p. 10.

[38] S. Richmond, "Once Again: Art Education, Politics, and the Aesthetic Perspective," *Canadian Rev. of Art Education* 16 (1989): 119.

[39] Dimondstein, "The Place of Dance in General Education," p. 82.

[40] Ibid., p. 83.

Chapter II

The Aesthetic Nature of Creative Dance

In chapter one, I suggested that creative dance's strongest value lies in its potential as an aesthetic activity. But what does it mean for an activity to have an aesthetic nature? I referred to the aesthetic features shared by different art forms. But what are these aesthetic features? Is there agreement amongst aestheticians as to what is and what is not an aesthetic feature? Agreement on this topic may require prior agreement regarding a theory of aesthetics. A theory of aesthetics would illuminate the purpose of art – is it to imitate reality, express feelings, convey formal features? If aestheticians do not agree regarding the purpose of art and the features shared by works of art, does this mean that aesthetic activity lapses into a sphere of subjectivity? In this chapter, I consider these questions in an attempt to elucidate more fully what it means to refer to creative dance as an art form.

This chapter will involve an exploration of what we typically mean by the aesthetic, with reference to the features shared by works of art. This exploration will include an explication and critique of traditional aesthetic theories as well as an examination of which aesthetic theories make sense concerning creative dance. If we are to consider creative dance to be an aesthetic activity and if we are to justify its inclusion in the curriculum as an *educational* activity, then we must examine the possibility of an objective aesthetics. If one opinion regarding works of art is as valid as another, we would find it difficult to conceive of this situation as being conducive to an educational process. If aesthetic values *are* more than subjective opinion, it would be possible for students to improve their ability to understand and to create works of art and thus education in the arts becomes a valid enterprise. Judgment in appreciating and creating works of art involves reasoning. I will examine the form that this reasoning takes in chapter three.

An Aesthetic Nature

When we call an activity aesthetic in nature, we are typically referring to an activity or to the objects produced through such activity, which, in Crawford's words, "we find perceptually interesting and attractive – objects that can be valued not simply as means to other ends but in themselves or for their own sake."[1] Richmond defines the aesthetic "in its most widely accepted sense as a special kind of perceptual attitude or outlook that involves the apprehension of an object, natural or man-made for its own sake."[2] The notion of intrinsic value which recurs in definitions of the aesthetic finds something of a parallel in Stanley's discussion of movement. She makes a distinction between functional and expressive movement, where functional movement "may be defined as the type which is geared to accomplish a practical task."[3] We may infer that if expressive movement is not intended to accomplish a practical task, then its value is intrinsic rather than instrumental. However, movement which is expressive (or any other expressive activity, e.g., painting, writing, etc.) may be intrinsically valuable but it may also be justified based on the understanding which can be attained through participation in the activity. I will explore this issue further in chapter three, but at this point I will consider what makes an aesthetic activity "perceptually interesting and attractive."

Aesthetic Features

We consider an activity such as dance or an object such as a painting to be perceptually interesting and attractive if it shares certain features with other similar activities or objects. Reference to these features distinguishes art from other areas. Richmond illuminates this point in his discussion of the educational value of the arts. He argues

> *if art is to be differentiated from purely conceptual matters, from the pragmatic communication of information in images, or from social studies, for example, then it must surely be by some reference to aesthetic intentions and qualities, i.e., to such things as style, character, design, skillful use of materials, originality, expressiveness, and the fittingness of form with content. Art so distinguished is (uniquely) worthwhile educationally in as much as it provides inspiration for creativity and reveals for our understanding and appreciation imaginative and insightful images of reality in aesthetically significant visual form.*[4]

The suggestion that there are aesthetic features shared by different art forms has not gone uncontested. Sheppard states that "if we try to develop such an extension in detail we are immediately confronted by the problem that formal features in the different arts seem at first to be of very different kinds."[5] However, Sheppard notes that, in considering formal features of a work of art, one is considering relationships between features. "In discussing painting we talk not just about the shapes and colours used but about the balance and the symmetry of the composition, that is, about the relationships between the shapes and colours."[6] We can easily apply the features of balance and symmetry to creative dance. For example, a choreographer might create a dance which has an even number of dancers performing symmetrical movements on opposing sides of the stage. Likewise, a dance could convey imbalance and asymmetry by utilizing an odd number of dancers performing movements at various levels with varying degrees of intensity. The utilization of aesthetic features such as balance and symmetry (as well as other features such as unity, coherence, variety, rhythm, dynamics, contrast, transitions, sequence, proportion, harmony, climax, etc.) makes it possible to compare and contrast works of art in the same as well as in different art forms.

Although aesthetic features may transcend different art forms, some features play a more prominent role in some art forms than in others. Meynell suggests "that visual art excels in its clarification of sensation; that music excels in the depiction of mood; that literature is unique in its capacity to anatomise judgment and decision."[7] Meynell goes into more detail in comparing and contrasting different art forms by first suggesting features common to all art forms and then considering how the emphasis varies according to the specific art form under discussion.

> *Each type of art is a matter of manipulation of a medium (a) to provide a structure (b) which is a means to satisfaction through exercise and enlargement of consciousness. While representation is certainly not the only means by which such an end may be secured, it is at least characteristic of literature and the visual arts that they exercise and enlarge consciousness through representation (c); and that such representation is more deeply satisfying when it involves some kind of reference to what is of central importance in human life (d).*[8]

Regarding the specific artistic forms of literature, Meynell specifies the features deemed to be valuable.

> *When examining the criticism of novels, plays, and other works of literature, such works are deemed to be of value in proportion to (i) their illustration and demonstration of what is of central importance for human life; (ii) the originality of their use of language and their treatment of plot, character, situation, and so on; (iii) their just representation of people, things and circumstances; and (iv) their overall unity in variety of substance and effect. It will be seen that these features correspond respectively to (d), (a), (c) and (b) above.*[9]

Regarding works of visual art, Meynell suggests that they "are found to be of value in proportion to (as well, presumably, as their exploitation of their medium as such) (i) their enhancement of perception and imagination (often through representation); (ii) their emotional significance; (iii) their unity in variety – which correspond to (c), (d), and (b)."[10] Finally, regarding works of music, Meynell suggests that their value "is found to be a matter of (i) its exploitation of the medium of sound as such; (ii) the clarity and intensity of its depiction of emotion and mood; (iii) its unity in variety – which correspond to (a), (d) and (b)."[11]

Meynell considers the art forms of literature, visual art and music. Dimondstein performs a similar analysis, but she includes creative dance in her discussion.

> *Each art form has its own distinguishing characteristics, provides a unique image, and uses particular media. How, then, can we give the arts a sense of unity as well as recognize their distinctiveness? To do so is to consider them in their broadest context, as parameters of space-time-force through which the functions of the arts are expressed. As parameters, they may have various values, yet each in its own way is necessary in creating and determining the aesthetic effects of any particular form. They cannot, then, be conceived as technical elements, but as the connective tissue underlying the expression of ideas and feelings.[12]*

Dimondstein gives examples of how the same feature is expressed in different art forms. "When we speak of an energetic line or a strong color relationship in painting, of tension between the volumes or contours in a sculpture, of the power of a movement in dance or the intensity of an image in poetry, we are expressing a sense of vitality."[13]

Although the preceding discussion gives the impression that there are agreed-upon aesthetic features common to all art forms, we must be careful not to jump to the conclusion that we can come to understand these features apart from the works of which they are constitutive. Redfern makes this point

when she insists that "aesthetic concepts (that is, concepts functioning aesthetically) are not grasped intellectually and then applied over a variety of instances: appreciation of works even within the same art form requires judgment (in that sense which involves perception and thought in felt experience) *in each particular case.*"[14] The notion that aesthetic features are inseparable from the works of which they are constitutive finds a parallel in the age-old form versus content debate. Whether we can separate form from content and/or which one should be given priority immerses us in the realm of aesthetic theories, i.e., to what extent is the purpose of art simply to convey formal features or is the content of art an imitation of reality with formal features playing a secondary role. Thus, we must consider an examination of aesthetic theories.

Aesthetic Theories

Traditionally, scholars have proposed three main types of aesthetic theories: that the purpose of art is to imitate or represent reality; that the purpose of art is to express emotions; and that the purpose of art is to depict formal features. The theory that art is an imitation or representation of reality has a long history, dating back to Plato (he considers the painter imitating the form of a couch as being "three removes from nature."[15]) However there are weaknesses with this theory. As Sheppard points out, "the theory not only claims that imitation is what all works of art have in common but also makes this the criterion of their value."[16] Upon closer examination though, it becomes evident that imitation does not fully explain why art is valued.

> *Whether Constable's* The Hay Wain *looks like a real early nineteenth-century haywain, in a real setting, or like some ideal of an English country scene, we do not think we see a real haywain, a real river, and real trees before us on the wall of the National Gallery, confined by a canvas, and we may admire the painting for the skill of the composition, for the way the haywain on one side of the picture balances the cottage on the other, or for the soft colours, rather than as an imitation.*

> *Similarly, we may appreciate the skill with which a novel's plot is constructed, or the novelist's use of language, even if we do not find the characters 'true to life'. Imitation does not fully explain why we value works of art.*[17]

Thus, it would seem that we would have to take features such as composition and plot structure into account when evaluating works of art. Another weakness with the imitation theory of art is that not all works of art are imitative or representational. Although we could say that abstract art represents emotions or states of mind, using the term representation in this way may be somewhat tenuous. "Representation does play a part in our valuing of representational art but since not all art is representational it cannot be representation which explains the value of all art."[18]

A second theory which attempts to explain the value of works of art inexplicable by the theory of imitation is the expressi‌on ‌ression of the em ‌ ‌ it finds its great‌ ‌ ‌d Col- lingwood ‌ ‌ expres- sionism, ‌ ‌t is the externali‌ ‌. There are a num‌ ‌irst, an audience ‌ ‌artist's mind.

There i‌ ‌was other th‌ ‌ailed account ‌ ‌ould not help ‌ ‌than he cons‌ ‌that the acc‌ ‌el of concepti‌ ‌ ‌ was not a reliable guide to the artistic expression or intuition. But if we cannot know the artist's expression except through the work, it is misleading to maintain that what was in the artist's mind is more real or more valuable than the object he has produced.[19]

[Handwritten notes:]
- Expressionist theory – Purpose of art is to express emotions.
- Audience cannot know what is going on in the artist's mind.
- More plausible for some art forms than for others.
- Only one aspect of art.

Another weakness with the expressionist theory is that it is more plausible for some art forms than for others. "If I make up a tune, it can indeed exist 'in my head' without being written down and the notes in which I write it down can be thought of as only an aid to my recreating it in my head another time. With a painting on the other hand, its production in the medium of paint on canvas seems all important."[20] A final weakness, reminiscent of the imitation theory, is that expression is only one aspect of art. Even works we consider very expressive involve aspects of form which have to be taken into account. The involvement of aspects of form ushers in a consideration of the third main aesthetic theory – that of formalism.

According to Sheppard, modern theories of art as form developed out of expressionist theories. "A search for expression or expressiveness 'in' a work of art leads easily to a close concern with the details of the work itself, including its form and structure."[21] In speaking of form, we are referring to relationships between features, i.e., the relationship between colors in a painting, notes in a piece of music, parts of a plot in a novel. The weakness of an aesthetic theory whose focus is strictly on form is that only a limited number of works could be called art. For instance, we would have to limit our concept of music to instrumental music, since the addition of lyrics introduces an element of representation. Our concept of visual art would be limited to abstract art since paintings of "things" also include an element of representation. Sheppard goes further to suggest that even abstract paintings involve a limited degree of representation.

> *In abstract paintings we do find just shapes and colours but even there one shape may appear to be behind another or shapes may seem to be moving across a picture. . . Canvases are in two dimensions while paintings are usually of things in three dimensions and in the recognition of a painted shape as three-dimensional some minimal element of representation is already creeping in.*[22]

She proposes that even if one could train oneself to see paintings as two-dimensional forms, one may not find them aesthetically interesting. "The use of form in Uccello's painting [The Battle of San Romano] is interesting precisely because he has represented in a very ordered way what would in reality be a chaotic scene. We should take much less interest in the picture if it were just a collection of blobs and lines."[23] Thus, just as theories of imitation/representation and expression need to take formal features into account, formalist theories cannot ignore elements of representation and the expression of the artist.

In conclusion, there does not appear to be one aesthetic theory which can provide a satisfactory account of the nature and value of art. Aestheticians have attempted to combine these theories but there seems to be no agreement as to whether the emphasis should be placed on the representative, expressionist or formal qualities of works of art. A theory of aesthetics which best describes what happens in creative dance would be a combination of the theories of representation, expressionism and formalism with an emphasis on expressionism. In chapter one I describe creative dance as the expression of thoughts and feelings through the medium of movement. Thus, although the expression of thoughts and feelings is central to creative dance, the medium of movement involves elements of formalism. In addition, it is possible that some of the expressive movements may represent reality to some degree, and thus, this expression would involve elements of representation or imitation.

Some may contest such an emphasis on expression in creative dance. That is, they may raise the question as to whether creative dance is always expressive in nature. To answer this question, we must first consider what we mean by expressive. When we suggest that the creative dancer expresses a thought or feeling through movement, this could be taken to mean that the dancer: 1) has that thought or feeling, 2) conveys, through the medium of movement, a thought or feeling, or 3) evokes in the audience a particular thought or feeling. What happens in art is expression in the second sense. That is, the creative dancer takes a thought or feeling and gives form to it, utilizing elements of movement to reach this end. This process does not require that the dancer experience the particular feeling being expressed. Rather, the dancer has objectified that feeling, thereby making the expression something independent from him/herself. The audience, upon perceiving the dance piece, may "feel" the feeling being expressed but they need not. However, if the dance piece is to result in an aesthetic experience, the audience should "feel" what the dancer has tried to express. This feeling will be intimately connected with an understanding of the expression, both its content, i.e., the feeling or thought, and the form, i.e., the movement elements as well as aesthetic features. Some may raise the question as to whether dance can be aesthetic without expressing a thought or a feeling. In fact, formalists would suggest that a dance performance concerns itself purely with the dancers' movements, nothing else. This conception of dance can be contested. Dancers may not always express particular feelings through dance, but when they are moving for the sake of movement, they may be expressing thoughts pertaining to the joy of pure movement. Thus, we can perceive creative dance as always involving the expression of thoughts or feelings through movement.

An Objective Aesthetics?

Many consider aesthetic activity to be subjective activity. A discussion of this issue has important implications for arts education. If aesthetic values are purely a matter of subjective opinion, one would be hard pressed to justify the inclusion of the arts in the curriculum as an *educative* activity. One opinion regarding works of art would be as valid as another and it would be difficult to conceive of this situation as being conducive to an educational process. On the other hand, if aesthetic values are more than subjective opinion, i.e., if there are interpretations or expressions of works of art which are more appropriate than other interpretations or expressions, it is possible for students to improve their ability to understand and create works of art, and thus education in the arts becomes a valid enterprise. Thus, it is of fundamental importance that art educators explore the issue of whether aesthetic values are in some sense objective.

At this point, I feel it important to clarify what is meant by "subjective" and "objective." It is helpful to view these concepts as two ends of a continuum. At the subjective end we have judgments based upon ourselves as subjects. That is, such judgments are based upon personal feelings. Some of them like "I feel sick" are non-debatable, while others such as "I feel that arts courses should be given preferred time slots in the curriculum" display a personal bias. Personally biased judgments are typically utilized as ammunition by those criticizing the arts as being a subjective activity and are considered to be idiosyncratic to particular individuals.

At the other end of the continuum, we have judgments based upon the properties of objects. Traditionally, such judgments were seen to be the domain of the sciences. Scientists would observe "facts" about the universe and make judgments based upon them. However, the recent work of epistemological theorists and philosophers of science (for example, Kuhn and Feyerabend), has demonstrated that there are no such facts. Every observation is "theory-laden" to some extent. That is, how we observe the world is based to a large degree upo[n] ... t the time. The di... and after the C... f the "theory-lad[en] ...

Thus, we ... continuum an[d] ... tate- ments invol... I feel that the art[s] ... ts in the curricul... f the arts. By cor... table because the ... can demonstrat... often consider art ... e, in which one o... that

[Handwritten annotation overlaid on text:]
- Subjective – Judgements based upon personal feelings.
- Objective – Judgements based on the properties of objects.
  ↳ Theory-laden facts

artistic judgments are debatable, that they are more like the "I feel that arts courses should be given preferred time slots in the curriculum" statement which can be judged against various accounts of the value of the arts. The position which artistic judgments occupy on the objective-subjective continuum is the topic of the next section.

The Objective-Subjective Relationship

Although aesthetic activity may not fall as far towards the objective end of the objective-subjective continuum as scientific activity, aesthetic activity should not be relegated to the purely subjective end. The notion that there is some middle ground between pure subjectivity and complete objectivity is reiterated by Rader and Jessup:

> Subjective value is a property of subjects and objective value is a property of objects; but neither, in isolation, is the entire value. The whole relational complex, I-R-O ["I" is the interest of the subject, "O" is the object of the interest, and "R" is the relation between them], is the only actual and complete value. The two opposing theories – subjectivism and objectivism – represent partial truths, and the whole truth combines the valid insights of both.[24]

Macdonald also denies the objective-subjective dichotomy when he suggests that "aesthetic judgment is not a matter of 'either-or,' with pure subjectivity (a chaos of personal opinion) on the one hand, and the complete objectivity claimed by science on the other hand."[25] Macdonald explains the subjective criterion of aesthetic judgments as entailing the pleasure-giving quality of a work of art. "If the individual does not find the work of art, be it a picture, a piece of music, a statue, or a poem, interesting and worth contemplating on its own account, then for him that work is not functioning as art."[26] However, the more objective criterion of aesthetic judgments involves, according to Macdonald, the quality of significance or depth of a work of art. ". . . the measure in which his [the artist's] work possesses the quality of significance yields a standard, and by no means a purely personal standard, for assessing the value of his product. This means in effect that the 'public' test is applicable, though not of course with the clarity and finality attaching to it in the sphere of science."[27] Macdonald adds the caveat that his "public" test does not involve the "clarity and finality" attached to science. By this, I take him to mean that there is something between "a purely personal standard" and scientific standards.

Another attempt to clarify the concept of objective, and thereby explain how aesthetic judgments can be classified as objective, is made by Meynell. He makes reference to two senses by which a judgment could be considered objective; he refers to these senses as 'A-objective' and 'B-objective'. Meynell considers a judgment to be A-objective if it is concerned with what is the case about objects apart from their actual or potential effects on human beings. He considers a judgment to be B-objective if it can be more or less verified or falsified in the experience of conscious subjects. Meynell suggests that typical scientific judgments are both A-objective and B-objective; "i.e., they can be more or less verified or falsified in the experience of conscious subjects and they refer to what might have been the case even if such experiences and the subjects enjoying them had never existed."[28] Aesthetic judgments, on the other hand, are certainly not A-objective; "they are about objects in their actual or potential relation to intelligent, sensitive subjects, and not about objects as they might have been even if such subjects had never existed."[29] According to Meynell, this distinction between A-objective and B-objective allows for the possibility of aesthetic judgments being both objective and subjective.

> *It may be inferred from what I have said that there is a sense in which both those who have argued for the objectivity and those who have argued for the subjectivity of aesthetic judgments are correct; the former in asserting their B-objectivity, the latter in denying their A-objectivity. Aesthetic judgments are 'subjective' in that their validation is entirely a matter of the actual or potential effect of the things concerned on the satisfaction of human subjects; they are 'objective' in that they can thus be shown to be true or false, quite independently of the*

attitude which may happen to be expressed by those who make them in the making of them.[30]

Can aesthetic judgments be shown to be true or false to some degree? I answer in the affirmative but this necessitates moving aesthetic judgments nearer to the "objective" end of the subjective-objective continuum. At this end, judgments are based upon the properties of objects – in this case, art objects. These properties would include such aesthetic features as line, design, color and shape, and the relationship between these, as well as the fittingness of this form to the content being expressed. These features are independent of particular persons experiencing works of art. Thus, we have a degree of objectivity. However, the application of this knowledge is intimately tied to the thoughts and feelings of the persons experiencing the art. Thus, there is still a degree of subjectivity. I must emphasize that the degree of subjectivity is not as extreme as undebatable "I feel sick" statements. As Bailin points out:

Aesthetic judgments do not reduce to personal preferences. Rather, they refer to objective features of works – their aesthetic properties, and to aesthetic principles. Thus, it is possible for there to be assessments of works of art which are unjustified, just as there are unjustified scientific judgments. It is, then, an intimate interplay of rational judgment and sensibility which is operating in the valuing of works of art.[31]

Once people are familiar with aesthetic features (they may not necessarily agree upon the importance placed upon any particular feature), they have something with which they can communicate their impressions to others experiencing the same work of art. Thus, if I feel that a particular painting leaves me feeling cold, I can point to the icy blue colors and the sharpness of the brush strokes used to apply those colors. Others may not interpret the painting in this way. In fact, they may say that the image the artist is representing is not one conducive to an interpretation of coldness. However, we are able to utilize talk of aesthetic features to provide reasons for our interpretations. Another example of this form of reasoning is literary criticism. When interpreting works of literature, scholars will argue for different interpretations based upon textual evidence. This evidence involves aesthetic features such as literary design, dramatic irony, figurative language, etc. Providing reasons based on such aesthetic features negates the possibility of aesthetic judgments being purely subjective. These reasons utilize a body of knowledge which is independent of the people applying it. This is where the objectivity lies.

The preceding example of literary criticism is illuminating not only for the aesthetic features scholars utilize in such criticism, but also for the role such criticism plays in the field of hermeneutics. Although scholars utilizing hermeneutic techniques may not refer to objective judgments, they do speak in terms of intersubjectivity. The sense of objectivity which exists in the realm of aesthetic judgments is related to this concept of intersubjectivity. In contrast to "scientific" objectivity, where the individual subject disappears as a determining point of reference, Peirce defines truth not in terms of subjectivity but rather intersubjectivity, "since an emerging consensus among the community of investigators is needed to cancel out what remains in an opinion of the accidental and arbitrary."[32] The possibility of objective "opinions" is reiterated by Habermas who "holds the view (stemming from Peirce) that we should think of objectivity as the quality of a set of opinions that can be successfully argued."[33] Although hermeneutic concepts will be referred to again in chapter three, at this point it is necessary to further explore the reasons utilized in arguing for a "quality set of opinions."

Ducasse questions the suggestion that aesthetic judgments are in some sense objective due to the nature of the reasons given for one's interpretation of a work of art.

But of what nature are those reasons? They are, ultimately, of the same nature as would be that offered by a man arguing that my pen had to fall when I let go of it a moment ago, because of gravitation. Gravitation is but the name we give to the general fact that unsupported objects do fall, and at a certain rate; but it is not a reason, or cause, or proof of that fact. To say that something always happens, is not to give any reason why it ever does. Therefore when I say that a certain design is ugly because it is against the "law of symmetry," I am not giving a reason why it had to give me aesthetic displeasure, but only mentioning the fact that it resembles in a stated respect certain others which as a bare matter of fact also do displease me. This character which displeases me and many persons, may, however, please others. And, what is more directly to the point, it not only may but it does, – jazzy or uncouth though I may call the taste of such persons.[34]

The key to responding to Ducasse's objection lies in his use of the concept of "taste." Ducasse has failed to distinguish between the pleasure or displeasure that persons experience, i.e., a reflection of their taste, with the reasons which they offer for a particular interpretation of a work of art. One example of this distinction is in the situation where two people agree on an interpretation of a work of art and may even provide similar reasons for their views. However, be this as it may, one person may like the work while the other dislikes it.

Morawski reiterates this distinction between taste and judgment. Morawski defines "taste" as "a certain disposition and the actual experiences connected with it, which are *not* identical with aesthetic judgment. This disposition belongs to the sensibilities and the imagination, which produce a specific and immediate response to some objects or qualities in a context which might be termed 'aesthetic'."[35] Morawski does not consider a taste response to be of an intellectual character. He explains such responses as rooted in one's natural dispositions as well as in one's cultural evolution. However one accounts for a taste response, Morawski notes the distinction between that and an aesthetic judgment response.

Aesthetic judgment proper is more remote from the taste experience, since it invokes some objective reasons to justify why "I like this" or, to restate it, why "X is likable." In this instance thought processes are intensified and the initial existential propositions to the effect that such are my feelings or that such are my sentiments towards the given object yield to implicational utterances or even to comparative formulas describing my experiences as compared with the feelings of others or describing the qualities or objects actually experienced as compared with those experienced on other occasions. In each of these latter cases, aesthetic judgment is an appraisal, that is, a statement ascribing for certain reasons some values to the experience, to its objective counterpart, to the adequate relation between them, or to some context in which such a relation might appear.[36]

Invoking objective reasons, as will be suggested in chapter three, grants aesthetic activity a place amongst other activities considered important for helping foster understanding of the human experience.

In conclusion, the main emphasis of creative dance involves expressing thoughts and feelings through movement. Also, art is not merely subjective, involving only personal feelings and expressions, but a sense of objectivity is possible. Finally, the judgments involved in both appreciating and creating works involve reasoning. I will examine the form this reasoning takes in the following chapter where I suggest that understanding is fostered through participation in creative dance.

Notes

[1] D. Crawford, "The Questions of Aesthetics," in R. Smith and A. Simpson, eds., *Aesthetics and Arts Education* (Urbana, Illinois: University of Illinois Press, 1991), p. 18.

[2] S. Richmond, "Once Again: Art Education, Politics, and the Aesthetic Perspective," *Canadian Review of Art Education* 16 (1989): 119.

[3] S. Stanley, *Physical Education: A Movement Orientation*, 2nd edition (Toronto: McGraw-Hill Ryerson, 1977), p. 33.

[4] S. Richmond, "Three Assumptions that Influence Art Education: A Description and a Critique," *Journal of Aesthetic Education* 25 (1991): 5.

5 A. Sheppard, *Aesthetics: An Introduction to the Philosophy of Art* (Oxford: Oxford University Press, 1987), p. 50.

6 Ibid.

7 H. Meynell, *The Nature of Aesthetic Value* (Albany: State University of New York Press, 1986), p. 29.

8 Ibid., p. 45.

9 Ibid.

10 Ibid.

11 Ibid., pp. 45-46.

12 G. Dimondstein, *Exploring the Arts with Children* (New York: MacMillan Publishing Co., 1974), pp. 30-31.

13 Ibid., p. 32.

14 H. Redfern, "Aesthetic Understanding," in Smith and Simpson, eds., *Aesthetics and Arts Education.*

15 Plato, *The Republic*, Book X, 597.

16 Sheppard, *Aesthetics*, p. 7.

17 Ibid.

18 Ibid., p. 17.

19 Ibid., pp. 25-26.

20 Ibid., p. 24.

21 Ibid., p. 41.

22 Ibid., p. 46.

23 Ibid., p. 47.

24 M. Rader & B. Jessup, *Art and Human Value* (New Jersey: Prentice-Hall, Inc., 1976), p. 15.

25 J. Macdonald, *A Philosophy of Education* (Toronto: W. J. Gage Ltd., 1965), p. 43.

26 Ibid., p. 43.

27 Ibid., p. 46.

[28] Meynell, *The Nature of Aesthetic Value*, p. 8.

[29] Ibid., p. 8.

[30] Ibid., p. 10.

[31] S. Bailin, *Achieving Extraordinary Ends: An Essay on Creativity* (Dordrecht: Kluwer Academic Publishers, 1988), p. 55.

[32] R. Howard, *Three Faces of Hermeneutics* (Berkeley: University of California Press, 1982), p. 102-103.

[33] Ibid., pp. 114-115.

[34] C. Ducasse, "The Subjectivity of Aesthetic Value," in J. Hospers, ed., *Introductory Readings in Aesthetics* (New York: The Free Press, 1969), pp. 297-298.

[35] S. Morawski, *Inquiries into the Fundamentals of Aesthetics* (Cambridge, Massachusetts: The MIT Press, 1974), p. 161.

[36] Ibid., pp. 163-164.

Chapter III

Fostering Understanding Through Creative Dance

In chapter one, I alluded to the possibility of fostering understanding of the human experience through creative dance. I will explore this possibility in more detail in this chapter. Furthermore, I will suggest that the understanding attained through participation in creative dance in particular and the arts in general is a particular sort of understanding, a rich understanding. In proposing that understanding can be attained through participation in the arts, we must give attention to the criticism that participation in the arts is being viewed as instrumentally, as opposed to intrinsically, valuable. Although art may be intrinsically valuable, the strongest justification for the inclusion of the arts in general, and creative dance in particular, in the educational curriculum relies on the ability of aesthetic activity to foster a rich understanding of the human experience.

A focus on the form of artistic expression results in the potential for attaining a rich understanding. The possibility of attaining understanding presupposes that aesthetic activity has a certain degree of objectivity. Although I argued for the existence of this objectivity in chapter two, we must now examine the sort of reasoning involved in appreciating and creating works of art. The reasoning involved in aesthetic activity has the potential to foster a rich understanding of the human experience. Having argued for the attainment of a rich understanding through aesthetic activity, I will justify the inclusion of creative dance in particular, as opposed to or in addition to other aesthetic activities. However, we must first examine aesthetic activity in general.

Intrinsic Versus Instrumental?

Theorists have justified aesthetic activity based on the intrinsic value inherent in such activity. Proponents of the "art for art's sake" point of view suggest that participation in aesthetic activity is valuable in and of itself; i.e., that appreciating and creating art is valuable for its own sake. This may be the case, but I must make two points in response to the "art for art's sake" position. First, if by "art for art's sake" we mean that appreciating and creating a work of art is pleasurable for its own sake, we must question this justification in an educational context. Justifying art for the pleasure it elicits would lead us down a slippery slope. What if students find encounters with comic books, or worse, pornography, to be pleasurable; does this justify *their* inclusion in the educational curriculum? Rather than justifying the inclusion of the arts on their pleasure-giving potential, it would be more prudent to examine their potential for expanding students' understanding. Ironically, Richmond (who is a strong advocate of the intrinsic value of art), suggests that "art so distinguished is (uniquely) worthwhile educationally in as much as it provides inspiration for creativity and *reveals for our understanding* and appreciation imaginative and insightful images of reality in aesthetically significant visual form" [italics added].[1]

The second point I must make is related to the ability of art to expand students' understanding. There cannot truly be "art for art's sake" but rather, in Abb's words, "art for meaning's sake."[2] By "art for meaning's sake," he is referring to the potential for students to derive meaning from encounters with art. I will explore this possibility in more detail in the next section. At this point, it is sufficient to note that to the degree to which works of art express content, they are instrumentally, not simply intrinsically, valuable. Richmond does not concur with this contention, making the distinction

> *between those who argue for the study of an apolitical, aesthetically autonomous art and those who see art in education as an avenue for asserting certain socio-political concerns, for example, Marxist or feminist, and various kinds of community action while denying lofty aesthetic ideals in favour of more popular and accessible art images.*[3]

Richmond's description of "those who argue for the study of an apolitical, aesthetically autonomous art" requires further analysis. Is it possible to have "apolitical, aesthetically autonomous art?" Although all art may not be political, all art expresses some content. Richmond would agree with this notion, for in an earlier paper he states that "content is necessary to art and to our pleasure in it in that artistic expression *always expresses something,* however abstract" [italics added].[4] The expression of content in art negates the possibility of "aesthetically autonomous art." This content need not be a blatant political statement, but it may be, depending on the "things that matter" to the artist. Richmond himself suggests that the educational value of art "resides in the discipline's capacity to develop the skills, sensibilities, and language of form needed to help students aesthetically express ideas and feelings about *the things that matter to them and to others in the community,* and to understand and appreciate the art around them" [italics added].[5] Marcuse emphasizes this notion of "things that matter" when he suggests that

> *Nevertheless society remains present in the autonomous realm of art in several ways: first of all as the "stuff" for the aesthetic representation which, past, and present, is transformed in this representation. This is the historicity of the conceptual, linguistic, and imaginable material which the tradition transmits to the artists and with or against which they have to work . . .*[6]

The "stuff" for aesthetic representation may be political, religious, cultural, etc.

The question which is certain to arise at this point is "what then separates art from propaganda?" Recall the description by Richmond of "those who see art in education as an avenue for asserting certain socio-political concerns, for example, Marxist or feminist, and various kinds of community action while denying lofty aesthetic ideals in favour of more popular and accessible art images."[7] This description illuminates the underlying dichotomy; on the one hand, there are "popular and accessible art images" and on the other, "lofty aesthetic ideals." However, these are not always, and need not be, exclusive. Part of the problem is a misunderstanding of the concept of aesthetic ideals. These need not be "lofty" and inaccessible to the general populace. In fact, if we understand the aesthetic in the manner defined by Abbs (i.e., " a mode of apprehending through the senses the patterned import of human experience"[8]) the distinction between the aesthetic and the accessible appears much less obvious. Although some people may need help in noticing the "patterned import of human experience," once some "tools" have been provided, i.e., "pointing out features such as line, design, colour, etc.," anyone who can "apprehend through the senses" can access the aesthetic.

The key to answering the question regarding the distinction between "popular and accessible art images" and propaganda lies in an understanding of the aesthetic in the terms proposed by Abbs. Critical in the definition of the aesthetic is the notion of "the *patterned import* of human experience." Apprehending the "patterned import" involves apprehending the aesthetic features discussed in the previous chapter. Not all sharing of the concerns of human experience can be apprehended aesthetically. There must be some pattern or form. Richmond points out the importance of form in aesthetic experience.

Under the aesthetic perspective, art is never considered simply as the communication of literal meaning, as the vehicle of social ideologies, or as text. What principally matters is an artwork's

> *unique qualitative character, and this leads inevitably to an*
> *interest in form, in relationships, in the way something is*
> *structured and shaped.*[9]

Thus, what distinguishes art from propaganda is this "interest in form, in relationships, in the way something is structured and shaped." I must emphasize that there is no sharp distinction between content and form. In fact, we cannot have one without the other. As Bailin points out "the manner of expression in art constitutes a part of what is expressed, and it is impossible to totally isolate either form or content."[10] However, we can pay greater or lesser attention to the form of an expression and what distinguishes propaganda from art is that with propaganda, we consider the message or content to be more important than the form in which it is expressed.

Returning to the original division "between those who argue for the study of an apolitical, aesthetically autonomous art and those who see art in education as an avenue for asserting certain socio-political concerns," it should be evident that the dichotomy underlying this division is false. There is no such thing as "aesthetically autonomous art" if we see art as an expression of human experience. On the other hand, we cannot view art as simply "an avenue for asserting certain socio-political concerns" if it is at all concerned with form, that is, how the content is expressed. The dissolution of this dichotomy by illuminating the emphasis on both form and content in art is necessary for a justification of aesthetic activity based on its potential for fostering understanding.

Understanding Through Content and Form

I intended the preceding discussion to demonstrate that to the degree that works of art express some content, they may be instrumentally, not simply intrinsically, valuable. Also, to the degree that works of art express such content, an argument to the effect that they promote understanding may appear unnecessary. Most people would agree that it is possible to understand the content of a work of art. However, to provide a complete justification for aesthetic activity, the question may be asked whether *how* the content is expressed (i.e., its form) has anything to do with understanding. That is, does one come to understand something by experiencing the form of a work of art? The answer is yes and furthermore, the understanding gained from experiencing how the content of a work of art is expressed is a rich sort of understanding. A demonstration of the possibility of attaining a rich understanding of the human experience through participation in the arts would provide a justification for the arts as a unique subject area, in the sense that only through aesthetic activity could this understanding be attained.

The suggestion that the form of artworks is essential to attaining a rich understanding through participation in aesthetic activity is related to what Abbs referred to as the sensuous, when he described the aesthetic as "a particular form of sensuous understanding."[11] The apprehension of the sensuous is a necessary condition for having an aesthetic experience. However, such perceptive experiences, be they visual, oral, tactile, etc., are not sufficient for an aesthetic experience to occur. Also needed for an aesthetic experience is the involvement of feelings on the part of the participant. This involvement of feelings is part of the sensuous in the definition of aesthetic as sensuous understanding. Note the linguistic connections between sensation and feeling. Abbs provides some illuminating illustrations. "'To keep in touch' is both to keep in contact and to remain close in feeling. To *touch* an object is to have a perceptual experience; *to be touched* by an event is to be emotionally moved by it. To have a *tactile* experience is to have a sensation in the finger-tips; to show *tact* is to exhibit an awareness of the feelings of others."[12]

Both the employment of the senses and the experiencing of feelings are necessary for an aesthetic experience to occur. The final condition necessary for an aesthetic experience is understanding, that is, Abb's "sensuous *understanding*." The apprehension through the senses (including feeling) makes it possible to attain sensuous understanding of the human experience. Continued apprehension leads to greater understanding of the human experience. An example of this sort of greater or enriched understanding also occurs in personal relationships. "Falling in love" with someone could easily fall into the immediate response category. However, the concept of "being in love" grows from this immediate response. As one spends time with, i.e., apprehends, one's lover, understanding of what it means to love grows; that is, the understanding becomes richer. This knowledge through acquaintance and experience is analogous to what happens when we apprehend a work of art. It may appear that comparing relationships between lovers with the relationship between art and its audience would take us further from, rather than closer to, providing a justification for aesthetic activity based on understanding. However, such a comparison illuminates the rich understanding attainable through aesthetic activity.

This knowledge by acquaintance is a term coined by Russell. Russell suggests that "we have acquaintance with anything of which we are directly aware."[13] This notion of "direct awareness" is reminiscent of Abb's definition of the aesthetic as "a mode of apprehension through the senses."[14] In fact, Russell suggests that sense-data supply the most obvious and striking example of knowledge by acquaintance. However, we are directly aware of more than just sense-data. According to Russell

> *all knowledge of truths, as we shall show, demands acquaintance with things which are of an essentially different character from sense-data, the things which are sometimes called 'abstract ideas,' but which we shall call 'universals'* . . . *that is to say, general ideas, such as* whiteness, diversity, brotherhood, *and so on.*[15]

We can come to know such universals by acquaintance with works of art. For example, the audience of a dance performance could come to understand the "universal" of *diversity* through being "acquainted" with the image of dancers moving in different and diverse ways. I must emphasize that, although the audience may become acquainted with *universals*, this acquaintance is the result of an encounter with a *particular* work of art. I will further discuss the possibility of attaining an understanding "beyond the particular" through the particular in the section entitled "Understanding as Feeling and Reasoning."

Suggesting that knowledge is attained through acquaintance with the arts leads to the question of whether this is simply private knowledge, not amenable to public debate. Hirst seems to hold this view when he states that he is interested in "knowledge by description" not "knowledge by acquaintance."

> *I am not here interested in the character of such personal experiences. It is rather the sense in which there is a content communicated in artistic expressions, and the legitimacy of talking here about knowledge of a propositional or statement kind that I wish to pursue. What is involved in the acquisition of any such knowledge is a further question.*[16]

However, the most promising justification for aesthetic activity lies in this "further question." Hirst, in introducing his paper "Literature and the Fine Arts as a Unique Form of Knowledge," suggests that "this [art as a unique form of knowledge] may be the least interesting, indeed the least important or valuable, aspect of the arts."[17] Hirst's suggestion would be correct if by knowledge one focuses only on a propositional kind, i.e., knowledge having to do with propositions as opposed to experiences. However, this narrow focus does not do justice to a discussion of the understanding which can be attained through acquaintance with the arts. Hirst attempts to discuss the possibility that works of art can be regarded as statements of a unique kind, but he sets aside questions about the nature of artistic experience. However, it is not possible to consider works of art as unique statements *without* questioning the nature of artistic experience. Hirst avoids discussing the very thing that makes artistic statements unique. "Artistic knowledge is autonomous because it involves elements over and above those derived from elsewhere, but no particular character for these elements is being suggested other than that they are essentially artistic."[18] A discussion of the character of these "elements" is necessary if a justification based on understanding is to have any strength. The primary character of artistic elements is their sensuous nature – involving both sensations and feelings.

Some are sure to criticize talk of sensations and feelings as involving only private knowledge. Underlying this criticism is a perceived dichotomy between private and public knowledge. However, this dichotomy is not as rigid as critics typically perceive it to be. Hirst refers to artistic concepts and their role in a public language.

An area of experience arises with the development of the concepts it employs and they in their turn develop in the use of the appropriate public language. Just as our experience of the physical world is determined by and limited by the concepts we have learnt in public discourse about that world, so our artistic experience will be limited by the mastery we have of the language that is art. But what is more, it is an essential part of this thesis that works of art are not conceivable as expressions of essentially non-artistic experience. The type of experience concerned and the type of discourse necessarily go together as they share the same concepts.[19]

Ironically, Hirst has "hit the nail on the head" regarding the dissolution of the private/public knowledge dichotomy. Artistic experience and artistic discourse "share the same concepts." Although artistic discourse may be public, artistic experience involves private feelings and sensations. However, these private sensations and feelings are understood and expressed through concepts which are part of a public language. For example, if someone is viewing Picasso's *Guernica*, he/she visually senses harsh lines, distorted figures, anguished features, etc. The concepts of harsh lines, etc., have been developed through a public language. The visual sensations described by these concepts, however, are inseparably tied to our feelings in viewing the painting. We may feel distressed, disgusted with what people do to each other through war. This understanding about war is enriched through experience with the painting. This understanding is different than the understanding attained when we are simply told that war has ugly consequences. By *feeling* the anguish in the faces of the figures represented, we understand the ugliness of war in a richer sense than if we are simply told this. However, this understanding is not confined to the private sphere. We can point out the distorted features (using public concepts) and others may feel what we feel. However, some may not feel the same disgust. These artistic concepts are necessary but not always sufficient for the attainment of a rich understanding of the context being expressed through the work.

Interpretive Reasoning

Suggesting the possibility of attaining understanding through acquaintance and experience with art is sure to elicit cries of "subjectivism." However, as I argued in chapter two, there is a sense of objectivity based on the utilization of a body of knowledge involving aesthetic features which is independent of particular people experiencing works of art. This body of knowledge makes it possible to provide reasons for making aesthetic judgments which are not purely subjective. Scholars typically levy the charge of subjectivism against the arts as a result of comparing the arts to science – the paradigm of rationality. Best notes this situation when he states that "what often impels people to subjectivism about the arts is the common assumption that the sciences are paradigm examples of rationality, coupled with the recognition that artistic judgments are obviously not open to scientific verification."[20] However, this comparison simply demonstrates that art is not science. Just because artistic judgments are not open to scientific verification, it does not follow that they are closed to all forms of verification. Moreover, contemporary philosophers of science have called into question traditional views concerning scientific verification and scientific objectivity.

A scientist cannot by himself explain something for himself alone. In order even to know "what" he is to explain, he must already have come to an understanding with others on the matter. As C. S. Peirce recognized, a semiotic community of interpretation always corresponds to the community of experimentation of natural scientists. Now, such an agreement on the intersubjective level can never be replaced by a procedure of objective science, precisely because it is a condition of the possibility of objective science; thus we encounter here an absolute limit to any program of objective-explanatory science.[21]

Intersubjective agreement makes it possible to have "objective" science and, as I argued in the previous chapter, that intersubjective agreement makes it possible to have "objective" artistic experience. However, this "objective" artistic experience requires a different form of verification.

More flexible forms of verification involve an exploration of different forms of reasoning. Besides the deductive and inductive reasoning characteristic of math and science, we can also use reasoning to give an interpretation or picture of a phenomenon or situation. Best cites Wittgenstein's duck-rabbit figure to illustrate how we can give reasons to support our interpretation; i.e., "see, it's a rabbit – here are its ears." However, Best aptly notes that "there is not the arbitrary unlimited possibility implied by subjectivism. The figure cannot be seen as a clock, for instance."[22] Best's comments concerning the limitations imposed on this sort of reasoning are important to keep in mind. Too often, critics perceive aesthetic judgments as "anything goes;" i.e., whatever a person subjectively thinks or feels about a work of art is correct. However, aesthetic features, such as the fittingness of form to content, provide a conceptual framework within which aesthetic judgments have something of an objective basis. Best suggests that "to decline to accept an interpretation of a novel or play for which the textual evidence is overwhelming and in the absence of countervailing reasons is a manifestation not of unfettered individuality but of a failure to understand the work and the relevant concept of art."[23] Individuality should not preclude the answerability to reason.

On the contrary, independent thinking in the arts as much as in science, mathematics and philosophy is not only compatible with but presupposes rationality. What is required is not conformity but that independent thought should be answerable

> *to valid reasons. In that sense rationality is a precondition of the individual differences in the creation and appreciation of the arts which are such significant expressions of the rich diversity in human personality. Although it is a fundamental misconception about this issue which is a major source of subjectivism.*[24]

In suggesting that individual thought is answerable to reason, we must not assume that everyone will agree upon the same interpretation of a work of art. "It follows from the meaning of 'interpretation' that disagreement is possible, and disagreement makes sense only by reference, if only implicit, to a shared conception."[25] Aesthetic features are the "shared conceptions" which make it possible to provide reasons for the interpretation of a work of art. People may not agree on an interpretation but, having acquired some knowledge of aesthetic features, they can convey their interpretations in such a way that others, although they may not agree, can at least understand the reasons for the interpretation. If the reasons are convincing, people may change their interpretation upon reflection on the various reasons presented. In this way, a person's understanding of a work of art may be enriched.

Understanding as Feeling and Reasoning

Although I have suggested that the charge of subjectivism does not hold and that aesthetic activity does involve reasoning, I have not yet considered the issue of how feelings relate to reason and how they too play a role in understanding. I will suggest that the traditional dichotomy between feeling and reason is a false one and that its dissolution is necessary for a justification based on understanding fostered through aesthetic activity. In other words, feeling, along with reason, is an integral part of sensuous understanding. Best gives a wonderful example of how the feeling involved in apprehending a work of art is integral in attaining a particular understanding. He quotes King Lear, wandering without shelter in a violent storm, and comments on how feeling contributes to Lear's understanding.

Poor naked wretches, whereso'er you are,
That bide the pelting of this pitiless storm,
How shall your houseless heads and unfed sides,
Your looped and windo'd raggedness, defend you
From seasons such as these? O! I have ta'en
Too little care of this. Take physic, Pomp;
Expose thyself to feel what wretches feel,
That thou mayst shake the superflux to them.

It is through feeling that Lear begins to understand the plight
of the poor. The feeling arises from a particular experience, and
it brings him to see what he had never before realized. It has to
be brought home to him in his feeling for a particular situation.
Through an involvement with a particular work of art, such as
King Lear, we can achieve a similar understanding. This is the
peculiar power of the possibility of learning through the arts,
and this is the principle reason for the central importance of the
arts in education. If enough people learned to understand, in
this sense, the plight of the unfortunate, we surely could not
continue to have so many homeless while others have even
several palatial homes . . .[26]

The images portrayed by the actors and the set designers, as well as the force of Shakespeare's words, may create a situation where the audience becomes "caught up" in the action and begins to empathize with the characters. In this case, the audience might empathize with King Lear and perhaps vicariously feel what he feels and come to understand what he understood through the experience. However, the quality of the images will affect the sensations experienced by the audience and these in turn affect the feelings evoked. If the actor portraying King Lear does not give a realistic performance, chances are that the audience will not become "caught up" and feel what he feels and in turn, understand what King Lear understood. Thus, it is the combination of the quality of the sensations and the feelings evoked which lead to the occurrence of an aesthetic experience which is intimately connected with understanding.

I must emphasize at this point that the quality of the sensations is dependent upon the aesthetic features of the work. Aesthetic features act as standards to enable one to distinguish between the valuable and the non-valuable work of art. A work of art is valuable when its aesthetic features are utilized to their fullest, that is, when the color, the lines, the symmetry, etc., are integral to the thoughts and feelings being expressed. In fact, in a valuable work of art, what the artist is expressing is inseparable from how it is being expressed. A verbal description of a painting is not expressing the same thing as the painting itself, and a written interpretation of a dance piece is not another way of expressing the same content. Bailin, in discussing Nussbaum's work on the ability of literary works to foster moral understanding, emphasizes the importance of contact with *good* literary works. "This is because the kind of perception at issue involves an accurate and nuanced grasp of particulars, a grasping of just the way things are, and such an understanding can be expressed only in the subtle, precise, and rich language that is the characteristic of good literature."[27] In other words, the subtlety, precision and richness of the language of *King Lear* is necessary for the play to express what it expresses. Thus, the aesthetic features found in *King Lear* contribute to the rich understanding which it is possible to attain through experience with the arts.

Another reason it is important to experience *good* art, i.e., art that is aesthetically valuable, versus just any expression, is that good art is, by definition, *original* and thus, it provides *new* insights. The possibility of attaining new insights from "formula" novels is highly unlikely. An over-use of clichés and highly predictable plots does not leave the reader with a new understanding of the human experience. *Good* art, on the other hand, captures the subtle nuances of the human experience, and these nuances may not have been noticed by the audience until they are encountered through the work of art. These "new" insights lead to a richer understanding of the human experience. In the next chapter, I will examine the importance of originality for fostering understanding through the *creation* of art, but at this point an emphasis is being placed on the importance of *appreciating* original works of art. Thus far, the discussion has concerned the arts in general, but I will now examine dance in particular.

I intended the preceding examples of *King Lear* and Picasso's *Guernica* to demonstrate both the feeling and understanding involved in apprehending works of art. However, most works of literature and some works of visual art are obvious examples of art forms having cognitive content. The proposition that creative dance has cognitive content may not be as obvious. However, an example of a dance piece will address this concern. Ruth Cansfield's work entitled "Balance" provides a good example of the rich understanding one can attain through experiencing the form of a dance piece. I will provide a description of this dance piece as well as an interpretation, recognizing that a description is an impoverished substitute for actually experiencing the dance.

The stage is dark. A spot light shines on upstage left. A dancer, dressed in a blue unitard, enters. Music is playing but more significant than the music are the dancer's movements. Most significant of the dancer's movements are the moments when she reaches for a position where she is unable to hold her balance. For a moment she seems to hold this position, but then the pull of gravity wins out and she topples over, only to try again and again. These movements continue for half of the dance; at which point, after losing her balance one last time, the dancer crawls off downstage. Without missing a beat of the music, another dancer, also dressed in a blue unitard, enters upstage. She proceeds to perform the same sorts of reaching and falling movements performed by the first dancer. However, the dance ends with the second dancer not crawling off the stage, but rather exiting in a "reaching" position.

The movements of the dancers (as well as the title of the piece) suggest an interpretation based on the theme of balance. More specifically, the dance could represent humankind's attempt to achieve balance, balance within our relationships with each other, the earth, ourselves. We witness the difficulty of achieving such balance in the effort displayed by the dancers in their attempt to hold their positions before toppling over. The continuous attempts of the dancers to regain balance after toppling over could be reflective of humankind's perseverance in achieving some sort of balance. The cyclical, ongoing nature of these attempts are illustrated by the entrance of the second dancer upon the exit of the first. The utilization of the same exit and entrance points emphasize the cycle involved. Finally, the dance ends on an optimistic note. Although the first dancer crawled off the stage, the final dancer left our view in a "reaching" position. Although one can visualize the second dancer not being able to hold her position, the fact that our last image of her is one of reaching rather than falling leaves us with a feeling of hope.

Although the dance is simple in design, much of its beauty lies in its simplicity. Having only one dancer on stage at a time allows the audience to focus on the movements; first the reaching, the holding and then, the falling. Although some form of these movements is repeated continuously and we are sure that the pattern will repeat itself, each sequence creates feelings of tension and hope. By feeling this tension, the audience may come to a better understanding of the need for balance in one's life and the perseverance needed to achieve it. The understanding of this need for balance has been attained in a much richer sense than if we simply told someone that humankind must find a balance in their relationships to each other, the earth, themselves. Thus, it is the form of dance, not simply a statement regarding balance, that leads to the attainment of a rich understanding.

It is possible that someone watching the dance piece *Balance* would propose a different interpretation of the dance. As I suggested in the previous section, everyone may not agree upon the same interpretation of a work of art. As I also suggested, if people have acquired some knowledge of aesthetic features, they can convey their interpretations in such a way that others, although they may not agree, can at least understand the reasons for the interpretation. If the reasons are convincing, people may change their interpretation upon reflection on the various reasons presented. The question at this point is how people's feelings play a role in this process of reasoning. For example, if someone does not interpret the dancer's "reaching" movements as expressing hope, this person will not "feel" the hope felt by the person who does interpret the movements in this way. However, if the person changes his/her interpretation, i.e., if someone points out the "reaching" movements, the person may come to "feel" the hope expressed in such a movement. In this situation, the person's feeling changes with a change of interpretation. Thus, the feeling is connected to the understanding and the understanding is richer because of this affective dimension.

It is tempting to suggest that one interprets a work of art and as a result of this interpretation, has a certain feeling. However, I must emphasize that this process of reasoning is not dichotomous from the feeling evoked. The two are integrally connected. A person may experience a work of art and "feel" something, but he/she may not have consciously formulated an interpretation of the work. However, upon reflection, he/she may formulate an interpretation which would account for the feeling evoked. Although someone might "feel" something through an encounter with a work of art and not have consciously worked out an interpretation, it would seem highly improbable that anyone who has some knowledge of aesthetic features and is in a "normal" emotional state, could experience a good work of art without "feeling." By limiting the work of art to a *good* one, I am suggesting that the work has the aesthetic features necessary for the audience to interpret the subtle nuances which result in the attainment of a richer understanding of the human experience.

Returning to particular examples of dance pieces or works of art or literature, I must make one more point regarding the role that feelings play in sensuous understanding. Although experiencing *particular* works of art evokes the feelings necessary for understanding, the feelings evoked are not limited to particular situations. In fact, the content of works of art typically deals with, in Richmond's words, "the things that matter to them [artists] and to others in the community."[28] There are bound to be some commonalities in the "things that matter" to the members of a community. Although it may be questionable as to how far one can extend the notion of community (i.e., to a global community), the sense of a common humanity makes it possible to understand beyond one's particular situation. In the preceding section, "Understanding Through Content and Form," I alluded to the possibility of attaining an understanding "beyond the particular" through the particular. Nussbaum emphasizes this notion in her discussion of aesthetic experience in literature.

For while they [novels] do speak concretely about human beings in their varied social contexts, and see the social context in each case as relevant to choice, they also have built into their very structure a sense of our common humanity. . . While it is extremely difficult, and frequently impossible, to assess intuitively, as a possibility for oneself, an ethical or religious treatise from an extremely different cultural tradition, novels cross these boundaries far more vigorously, engaging the reader in emotions of compassion and love that make the reader herself a participant in the society in question, and an assessor of what it offers as material for human life in the world. Thus in their very structure they contain the interplay between the evolving general conception and the rich perception of the particular; and they teach the reader to navigate resourcefully between these two levels.[29]

The above quotation illustrates the interplay between reason and feeling which can lead one to a rich sort of understanding. The ability of novels (and potentially other art forms) to "engage the reader in emotions" and make her "an assessor of what it offers as material for human life in the world" is evidence that feeling and reason need not be considered dichotomous and that the interplay between them leads to the attainment of a rich understanding. Thus, to deny students access to the arts is to, in turn, deny them access to the possibility of a richer understanding than is possible without interaction with the arts. To quote Richmond, "the study and practice of art is liberating to the extent that it enables students to visually interpret and understand experience, and to reach penetrating insights about human life and values."[30] To deny students the liberation involved in feeling and reasoning in the arts is to deny them their full potential as humans. Greene, in answering the question "what are artists for?" suggests that

> *Artists are for disclosing the extraordinary in the ordinary. They are for transfiguring the commonplace, as they embody their perceptions and feelings and understandings in a range of languages, in formed substances of many kinds. They are for affirming the work of imagination – the cognitive capacity that summons up the 'as if', the possible, the what is not and yet might be. They are for doing all this in such a way as to enable those who open themselves to what they create to see more, to hear more, to feel more, to attend to more facets of the experienced world.*[31]

"To see more, to hear more, to feel more, to attend to more facets of the experienced world" will lead students to a greater understanding of "the experienced world" than that achieved in an educational system which does not include artistic experiences. Thus, the preceding justification will add some weight to the scale with the hope of tipping it in favor of the inclusion of arts education as an integral part of the educational curriculum.

Understanding Through Creative Dance

If aesthetic activity does provide a richer understanding of the human experience than that achieved in other subject areas, and if creative dance is an aesthetic activity, the result is a justification for the inclusion of creative dance in the educational curriculum. However, the question might be raised: why creative dance as opposed to other forms of dance and then further, why dance as opposed to other arts activities? I am *not* suggesting that creative dance be included in the curriculum *instead* of other arts activities. However, because the visual arts are usually the focus (if not the only activities) in art class and the study of drama and literature often finds a niche in the language arts class, I must make a special plea for the inclusion of creative dance in the educational curriculum. Although creative dance *is* sometimes included in the physical education class (and I am *not* suggesting that it be removed from the gymnasium), we must recognize its aesthetic potential if justice is to be done to the teaching of creative dance.

Regarding the inclusion of creative dance as opposed to other forms of dance, I must review the continuum of dance forms discussed in chapter one. The ballet end of the continuum is perhaps best left to ballet schools since the years of training required to become proficient in this dance form cannot be accommodated in the already "pressed for space" school curriculum. Furthermore, and perhaps more importantly, the limited scope of this dance form to permit students to create their own products is a serious limitation for an educational curriculum. This limitation is applicable, to lesser degrees, to the dance forms of jazz, tap, folk, social and modern. Although it is possible for students to create a choreography from a prescribed set of movements, the time it takes to learn these sets of movements often minimizes the time left over for actually creating dance pieces. Participation in creative dance allows the greatest scope for the creation of dance pieces by the students. The ability to create as well as appreciate art is important in the experience of aesthetic activity, as I will demonstrate in the following chapter. Thus, we must give students the opportunity to create. I must emphasize that a creative dance program should involve creating *and* appreciating dance. Thus, there is a role for the other dance forms. Students should be given the opportunity to watch ballet, tap and modern, as well as participate in folk and social dances. However, these experiences should not take the place of creating dances. Rather they should provide, foremost, an opportunity for developing aesthetic appreciation, and in addition, tools for the students to understand the aesthetic, e.g., watching ballet could help students understand aesthetic features such as balance, line, symmetry, etc., as well as skills they could use in creating dance pieces, e.g., learning certain folk or social dance steps which they could incorporate into a creative dance. Thus, we could use other forms of dance in the educational curriculum, but the primary dance form should be creative dance, since this form allows the students to create dance pieces and this is an important part of aesthetic activity.

If we accept the argument that creative dance, as opposed to other dance forms, should be the primary form of dance included in the educational curriculum, the question might still be raised regarding the need for creative dance if the curriculum already includes the teaching of the visual arts, drama and literature. There is a twofold response. First, children (and adults) all have a need to express thoughts and feelings, but the medium through which they prefer to express themselves will differ. An artist with the inclination and ability to express him/herself proficiently in all media would be a rare occurrence. Rather, people find particular media with which they are comfortable and they develop their ability to express themselves in their preferred medium. Children should be given the opportunity to experiment with a variety of media. Thus, an educational curriculum which did not allow children the opportunity to experiment with using their bodies as a means of expression would be deficient.

We could view the opportunity for students to use their bodies as an artistic medium as an additional justification for the inclusion of creative dance in the educational curriculum. If one considers the learning domains to include the cognitive, affective and psychomotor, it would seem that the psychomotor domain is shortchanged in the educational cur-riculum. Apart from physical education, the focus of most subject areas is primarily on the cognitive and secondarily on the affective learning domains. Creative dance, however, in-volves all three domains. The involvement of the psychomotor domain would not seem to require any further argument and a major thrust of this book has been that creative dance as an art form involves feeling and understanding (the affective and cognitive domains).

A second reason for including creative dance as well as the visual arts, drama and literature is that if the arts provide a richer understanding of the human experience than that achieved in other subject areas, then the more exposure the students have to experience with artistic activity, the better. Thus, it is important that students have an opportunity to find artistic media with which they are comfortable, as well as being given the opportunity to spend more than peripheral amounts of curriculum time in artistic activity.

Notes

1 S. Richmond, "Three Assumptions that Influence Art Education: A Description and a Critique," *Journal of Aesthetic Education* 25 (1991): 5.

2 P. Abbs, "The Pattern of Art-Making," in P. Abbs, ed., *The Symbolic Order: A Contemporary Reader on the Arts Debate* (London: Falmer Press, 1989), p. 209.

3 S. Richmond, "Art and Politics in John Berger's Novel A Painter of Our Time," *Journal of Social Theory and Art Education* 11 (June 1991): 26.

4 S. Richmond, "Once Again: Art Education, Politics, and the Aesthetic Perspective," *Canadian Review of Art Education* 16 (1989): 121.

5 Richmond, "Art and Politics," p. 33.

6 H. Marcuse, *The Aesthetic Dimension* (Boston: Beacon Press, 1978), p.18.

7 Richmond, "Art and Politics," p. 26.

8 Abbs, "Aesthetic Education: An Opening Manifesto," *The Symbolic Order*, p. 1.

9 Richmond, "Once Again," p. 1.

10 S. Bailin, *Achieving Extraordinary Ends: An Essay on Creativity* (Dordrecht: Kluwer Academic Publishers, 1988), p. 36.

11 Abbs, "Aesthetic Education: An Opening Manifesto," p. 1.

12 Ibid., p. 3.

13 B. Russell, *The Problems of Philosophy* (New York: Oxford University Press, 1959), p. 46.

14 Abbs, "Aesthetic Education: An Opening Manifesto," p. 1.

15 Russell, *The Problems of Philosophy*, pp. 48 & 52.

[16] P. Hirst, "Literature and the Fine Arts as a Unique Form of Knowledge," *Knowledge and the Curriculum: A Collection of Philosophical Papers* (London: Routledge & Kegan Paul, 1974), p. 154.

[17] Ibid., p. 152.

[18] Ibid., p. 162.

[19] Ibid.

[20] D. Best, *Feeling and Reason in the Arts* (London: Allen & Unwin, 1985), p. 15.

[21] K. Apel, "Perspectives for a General Hermeneutic Theory," in K. Mueller-Vollmer, ed., *The Hermeneutics Readers* (New York: Continuum Publishing Company, 1985), pp. 330-331.

[22] Best, *Feeling and Reason in the Arts*, p. 19.

[23] Ibid., p. 47.

[24] Ibid., p. 62.

[25] D. Best, *The Rationality of Feeling* (London, The Falmer Press, 1992), p. 38.

[26] Best, *Feeling and Reason in the Arts*, pp. 183-184.

[27] S. Bailin, "Other People's Products: The Value of Performing and Appreciating," *The Journal of Aesthetic Education* 27 (Summer 1993): 64.

[28] Richmond, "Art and Politics," p. 33.

[29] M. Nussbaum, *Love's Knowledge: Essays on Philosophy and Literature* (Oxford: Oxford University Press, 1990), p. 96.

[30] Richmond, "Art and Politics," p. 33.

[31] M. Greene, "Art Worlds in Schools," in *The Symbolic Order*, pp. 215-216.

Chapter IV

To Appreciate and Create Works with Aesthetic Features

In the previous chapter, I argued that creative dance, as an aesthetic activity, could foster a unique understanding of the human experience. We must now examine what form dance education would have to take if it is to foster this unique understanding. To foster understanding, creative dance must involve the appreciation and creation of works with aesthetic features. I will contrast the approach of appreciating and creating works with aesthetic features with prevalent approaches of fostering creativity in dance education (and education in general). There is much conceptual confusion surrounding prevalent notions of creativity and I will suggest that creativity involves precisely the creation of original works with aesthetic features. Furthermore, much of the confusion regarding the idea of creativity in dance education is a result of conflating the imaginative with the creative. However, an analysis of imaginative activities will be the topic of chapter five.

I intended the examples of *Balance, King Lear* and *Guernica* in the previous chapter to demonstrate how appreciating such works could result in the attainment of a rich form of understanding. The implication of this argument for creative dance education is that part of the educational curriculum would involve appreciating works of art. However, I also argued in the previous chapter that creative dance should be the dance form of choice in the educational curriculum because creative dance allowed the greatest scope for the *creation* of dance pieces by the students. Although the *appreciation* of works of dance may not require further justification at this point, we still need to address the justification for the *creation* of dance pieces. Why is it important for students to create rather than just appreciate works of dance? The answer to this question requires a return to a discussion of the expressive nature of creative dance.

In chapter one, I stated Dimondstein's definition of creative dance as "the interpretation of a child's ideas, feelings, and sensory impressions expressed symbolically in movement forms through the unique use of his body."[1] This expression can foster a unique understanding on the part of the dancer. In order to express "ideas, feelings, and sensory impressions," one has to have an understanding of what one is expressing. However, this understanding need not be complete. In fact, it is often through attempts at expressing ideas and feelings through some medium that an understanding of these ideas and feelings crystallizes. Thus, in giving artistic form to the expression of ideas and feelings, the creator has the potential to attain a richer understanding of these ideas and feelings than he/she had before attempting to express them. For example, in the case of creative dance, if a student wants to express a feeling of insecurity, he/she must think of a way to convey such a feeling through movement. He/she may try out different movements, e.g., pulling extended limbs into oneself, slowly shrinking into a tight ball, etc. Through experimenting with such movements, the dancer may come to a richer understanding of what it means to feel insecure. The dancer may have to recall times when he/she has felt insecure or observed an insecure person. These thoughts, along with the movements inspired by them, may result in the dancer attaining a richer understanding of the concept of insecurity than he/she had before attempting to create a dance piece on that theme.

The suggestion that the dancer attains a richer under-standing as a result of expressing thoughts and/or feelings through the medium of movement (in the case of dance) finds support in Collingwood's idea that the artist does not know what he/she wants to express until he/she expresses it. "The artist has no idea what the experience is which demands expression until he has expressed it. What he wants to say is not present to him as an end towards which means have to be devised; it becomes clear to him only as the poem takes shape in his mind, or the clay in his fingers."[2] Collingwood goes on to say that "they [works of art] are made deliberately and responsibly, by people who know what they are doing, even though they do not know in advance what is going to come of it."[3] Howard refers to this situation as a paradox of creativity; "that the artist both knows and does not know what he is up to."[4] The artist (or in the case of a creative dance class, the student) "comes to know" through the experience of giving artistic form to thoughts and/or feelings. Although Col-lingwood may be correct in suggesting that the artist does not have a complete knowledge of what is going to come of his/her work, the artist must know when he/she has arrived at a result which is satisfactory. Maitland agrees that in some way, the artist must know where he/she is heading. "Other-wise, he would be unable to make aesthetically discriminating or relevant choices or to correct his mistakes."[5] To know when a resulting work is satisfactory requires a knowledge of stand-ards of the discipline within which the artist is working. That is, the creative dancer must be satisfied that the dance created meets certain standards, i.e., that effort qualities have been utilized to their fullest, that aesthetic features have been recog-nized and emphasized, etc. Thus, in exploring a thought and/or feeling in an attempt to express it through movement, the creative dancer must utilize knowledge of movement elements and aesthetic features. This knowledge, utilized in an attempt to create an original expression, leads to a richer understanding of the thought/feeling being expressed as well as a deeper understanding of the art form itself.

To foster understanding in participants in a creative dance class requires the creation of original works with aesthetic features. In chapter three, it was suggested that aesthetic features act as standards to enable one to distinguish between the valuable and the non-valuable work of art. Maitland gives an example of an artist making changes to a painting; "if he was articulate and willing, he would point to certain features of the paintings and explain why certain choices did not work and why the changes were better in relation to the emerging works of art and what he wants to achieve."[6] An example from a creative dance class may further elucidate the role of aesthetic features in fostering understanding. If students were asked to create a dance based on a piece of music, the results would be quite different if the task was given within the constraints of acknowledging aesthetic features, as opposed to creating "free-form" with no aesthetic requirements. In acknowledging aesthetic features, the students would have to listen carefully to the music. They would have to acknowledge features of the music, e.g., changes in tempo, changes in volume, etc. They could then perform movements which coincided with the features of the music, e.g., fast movements with fast music; or they could use movements which created a feeling of dissonance with the features in the music, e.g., light movements to heavy music. Working within the constraints of aesthetic features, however, helps foster the understanding both of the aesthetic features of music and movement, for example, as well as the feelings which can be created utilizing such features, e.g., the feeling of dissonance created by juxtaposing contrasting features. This understanding would not be developed if students simply turned on some music and moved to it. In chapter three, I referred to Abb's definition of the aesthetic as "a mode of apprehending through the senses the patterned import of human experience"[7]. It is giving the experience with the music a "patterned import" wherein lies the possibility of an aesthetic experience, and as I argued earlier, the possibility of attaining a rich understanding.

Knowledge and use of aesthetic features may be what Collingwood had in mind when he spoke of artists "knowing what they were doing." Once again, this knowledge of aesthetic features is necessary for expressing thoughts and feelings through movement, if this expression is to foster a greater understanding of the thoughts and feelings being expressed. Students can acquire knowledge of such aesthetic features through the appreciation of great works of art. Thus, there is an important connection between appreciating and creating in the creative dance class. I must emphasize that in appreciating works of art, these works are not limited to dance pieces. As I argued in chapter two, aesthetic features transcend different art forms. Thus, appreciating the imbalance in a visual work or the disharmony in a musical piece may help a dancer to understand the possibility of expressing imbalance through movement.

Having argued that the inclusion of aesthetic features is necessary if the form of an expression is to foster understanding, we must now examine the role of creating aesthetic works which are *original*. When referring to works which are original, I mean works which are new, not only to the student, but which also go beyond conventional ways of doing things in that particular context, e.g., six year olds could try to create dances which are not copies of what other six year olds do or repetitions of things they have seen. Some may argue that students beginning work in creative dance will not be able to create something significant in terms of the tradition. However, in *attempting* to create something new in terms of the tradition, i.e., synthesizing and extending existing knowledge and skills, understanding is being fostered.

An understanding of aesthetic features related to movement elements is necessary if students are to create dances which will enrich their understanding of the thoughts/feelings being expressed. The knowledge of aesthetic features and movement principles must be taught and I will suggest in chapter six that the knowledge of aesthetic features and movement principles, and skill in utilizing this knowledge, can best be developed *initially* through imitation. Great works of art, as well as the creative dance teacher, are important models for students to imitate. However, I must emphasize at this point that to limit creative dance activities to imitating role models (regardless of the greatness of these models) will not lead to the attainment of understanding. Students are expected to utilize the knowledge and skills learned to create their own dances. The reason for this is that, in creating an original dance piece, the dancer comes to a greater understanding of the thought/feeling being expressed; as well, in creating original works, the dancer pushes forward the discipline of dance. I will consider both the enriched understanding of the thought/feeling being expressed as well as the enriched understanding of the art form itself.

Creating an original dance piece, based upon some thought or feeling the dancer wishes to express, requires the dancer to move beyond mere imitation of works created by others. The aim of creating an original piece will help eliminate the use of cliché-type or over-used movements. The dancer will have to "dig deeper" into what he/she means by the thought or feeling being expressed. The dancer will also have to consider how others have expressed similar thoughts or feelings in the past. In creating an original expression, the dancer will have to stretch his/her understanding of the thought/feeling being expressed and this process will lead to a richer understanding of what he/she means by that particular thought/feeling. An example from a creative dance class will help illustrate this point. If the students are asked to create a dance which expresses the thoughts and feelings surrounding a funeral, they may be tempted to put together movements typically witnessed at a funeral, i.e., solemn movements, heads hung low, etc. In creating a more original dance piece, the students may have to analyze the feelings resulting from the death of a loved one, e.g., sorrow as well as anger, etc. They could perform movements which expressed contrasting feelings and the interplay between these feelings. Such an analysis and the working through of possible movements to convey these feelings will result in a richer understanding of these feelings.

Once again, I must emphasize that the dancer does not "create" in a vacuum. He/she utilizes knowledge of and skill in using movement elements and aesthetic features, but the dancer must synthesize, modify and extend this knowledge and skill if the expression is to be original. This process of synthesizing and extending knowledge and skill leads to a deeper understanding of the art form itself. In fact, an extension of the knowledge of and skill in utilizing movement elements and aesthetic features may push forward the discipline of dance. Bailin, in discussing art works which are valued because they are innovative, suggests that

> [t]hey innovate in such a way as to provide a new and viable direction in which the art can grow, and what is viable is determined by the state of the tradition and by the state of the society. Thus works which attempt to deal with new technical problems at a point where old problems have been exhausted, or works which respond, both through form and content, to changes in society, are likely to be effective, to be appreciated, and to be valued.[8]

The fostering of understanding would be a noncontentious aim for most, if not all, creative dance instructors. However, this understanding is typically thought to be achieved through the free expression of students' thoughts and feelings. In fact, this is what often transpires in creative dance classes in the name of fostering creativity; e.g. "this art form emphasizes creativity,"[9] "it stimulates and enriches the creative personality,"[10] "creative experience with bodily self is fundamental to education."[11] It is further believed that knowledge of the skills and techniques of the art and the requirement to create works with aesthetic value will stifle this creative expression; e.g., "This is creative dance, dance that is for children and comes from children. It's not our adult ideas and values imposed on them."[12] "In reality, we do not teach creativity; it is already there. Rather we nurture it as we would a tender seedling, fertilizing, watering, providing rich soil, adequate light – and above all, love and gratitude. The rest is their own growth."[13] "[T]here is something called 'educational dance.' This is different from children's dance geared toward performance, or the learning of material and techniques which are developed by adults."[14] However, knowledge of the skills and techniques of the art form and the requirement to create works with aesthetic value do not stifle creativity, but rather enhance it. Furthermore, since the understanding that is to be attained depends upon the works created having aesthetic value, then the aims of fostering creativity and fostering understanding through the arts coincide.

In order to establish the importance of knowledge and skills in fostering creativity and understanding, we must consider the view of creativity which underpins the free expression argument. There are a number of assumptions underlying this view. The first assumption is that creativity is something innate to persons; that is, all children have the potential to be creative. Thus, it is the job of the teacher to provide means whereby this innate creativity can be freed and expressed. The second assumption is that creativity is some sort of process. Descriptions of this process have focused on the mysterious and the non-rational. We require an explication and critique of both of these assumptions. An alternative view is that the term "creative" should be applied to a product. In proposing the criteria for a product to be deemed creative, it will become evident that the aims of fostering creativity and fostering understanding through the arts coincide. What follows is an explication and critique of the view that fostering creativity involves free expression.

Creative Persons

There are a number of problems with the view that children are innately creative. Firstly, when we conceive of creativity as something innate to persons, we must question what this "something" is. Is it an ability? An ability to do what? Secondly, if creativity is an ability which is innate, can we enhance it or can it be "lost" if a person doesn't use it? Thirdly, and perhaps most importantly, how do we know that students have this ability?

If creativity is an ability, we must raise the question: what is it that everyone has the ability to do (if creativity is something *innate*)? The most logical answer to this question is that being creative suggests the ability to create. If we now ask: what is to be created?, a logical answer is – a product. If we assume the ability to create products is innate, the question could be asked: is it possible to enhance the creation of products? We could enhance the creation of products if we assisted students in creating "better" products. Regarding the possibility of "losing" this ability, if students quit creating products, they may have "lost" this creative ability, or simply stopped using it. This suggestion brings us to the third problem – how does one know whether students have this ability? They may have "lost" it, or perhaps, they never had it. The only way we could determine if persons were creative would be by what they produced. I am not denying the possibility of applying the term "creative" to persons. However, the term can only be applied to persons *after* someone has deemed the resulting product to be creative. Bailin questions the view that creativity is a quality possessed by a person regardless of whether the person actually creates anything.

> *Even if a creative capacity existed, how would it be possible to know whether a person possessed such a capacity? If someone produces valuable works, then we can, of course, say in retrospect that she was capable of producing valuable works, that she had the capacity to do so. If she has not done so, however, then what would lead one to attribute to her a creative capacity? Perhaps she has created valuable works in the past. In this case, the production of a product in the past is the basis for the prediction of future production.*[15]

The suggestion that the production of a product is important may not find favor with those advocating the free-expression argument. However, if creativity is viewed as something innate, this "something" must refer to an ability of sorts. If this "something" is an ability to create, then something must be created. Some sort of product is an indicator of the ability to be creative. Whether this ability is innate cannot be answered, since if persons do not create anything, one cannot tell if they have lost this ability or if they never had it.

Creative Processes

Rather than focus on the creation of products, many free-expression advocates prefer to focus on a creative process, e.g. "I wish to talk about the process of dancing and not the product."[16] "Process talk" has focused on the mysterious and the non-rational. When teachers view the creative process as something shrouded in mystery, they are often referring to acts of inspiration. We must then raise the question regarding the possibility of "inspiring" inspiration in students. I will explicate and critique this possibility.

The role of inspiration in the creative work of artists and scientists has been considered of paramount importance by many philosophers, artists and scientists since the time of antiquity. According to Plato, "the poet is a light and winged and holy thing, and *there is no invention in him until he has been inspired* and is out of his senses, and reason is no longer in him: no man, while he retains that faculty, has the oracular gift of poetry" [italics added].[17] Plato considered the artist to be at the mercy of the Muses – the source of inspiration. "They [the artists] are simply inspired to utter that to which the Muse impels them, and that only."[18] This feeling of being at the mercy of the source of inspiration is reiterated by Mozart. In reference to his ideas, he writes "*whence* and *how* they come, I know not; nor can I force them."[19] Andre Marie Ampere, after whom the unit of electric current is named, remarked that "for some days I had carried the idea about with me continually. At last, *I do not know how,* I found it, together with a large number of curious and new considerations concerning the theory of probability."[20] The great mathematician, Karl Friedrich Gauss, recalled his efforts to prove a difficult theorem: "as a sudden flash of light, the enigma was solved."[21] For Tchaikovsky, "the germ of a future composition comes suddenly and unexpectedly."[22] This sentiment is echoed over and over again in the realms of both art and science.

For these creators, the source of inspiration may have been supernatural or spiritual, as evident in Jacques Maritain's contention that everything depends "on the recognition of the existence of a spiritual unconscious, or rather, preconscious, of which Plato and the ancient wise men were well aware;"[23] or the source of inspiration may be some unknown layer of the mind, as suggested by Koestler when he states that "in the creative act there is an *upward* surge from some unknown, fertile, underground layers of the mind."[24] Whether we view the source of inspiration as supernatural, preconscious, or simply an unknown layer of the mind, the notion of inspiration is shrouded in mystery. Some philosophers, for example J. P. White, simply write off the notion of creative inspiration as a "fairy story."[25] Others are less harsh, but realistic about the consequences of such an account. Weisberg suggests that "if creative achievements do indeed come about through great leaps of insight, brought about by extraordinary thought processes, in individuals who possess some unanalyzable quality called genius, then little more can be said."[26]

What can be made of this creativity-as-inspiration account? Although Weisberg suggests that little more can be said if we view creativity as an inspirational process, two points must be made. First, even if someone is inspired by something beyond him/herself and this results in the creation of a product, if this product is not original or valuable, would it still be considered creative? What are the criteria for something to be deemed creative? I will explore the answer to this question in the following sections of this chapter. Secondly, if the source of inspiration is beyond the control of the person creating something, is there anything that can be done to "inspire" this inspiration; that is, can a teacher intervene to influence the inspirational process? Although a teacher could be perceived as a "source" of inspiration, a recurring theme in the anecdotal accounts cited at the beginning of this section involved the mystery of from where and how the inspirations came. This situation does not seem amenable to an educational context. Thus, if creativity always and only involves some sort of mysterious inspiration, it would not make sense to regard such a process as an educational objective.

As well as the mysterious "inspiration" view of creativity, one finds teachers adhering to the creative process view advocated by the likes of de Bono. De Bono advocates the development of lateral thinking as opposed to strictly vertical thinking. According to this view, a person encounters a problem, suspends vertical thinking and adopts lateral thinking, generating new possibilities. He sees the suspension of vertical thinking as allowing for "non-rational" leaps of thought. Thus, the creative process is fostered by freeing people from the hold of conventional logic and conventional ways of doing things. Once the problem has been solved, the person resumes vertical thinking and evaluates the solution. Such dichotomous modes of thinking are questionable. As Bailin points out

> . . . *judgment is intimately involved throughout the process of creating. The initial perception of the problem and the determining of the general direction for solution are very much products of judgment. It is because one has considerable expertise in an area and is immersed in its intricacies that one develops the judgment that enables one to see a certain concatenation of phenomena as in need of exploration or explanation, to see it as a problem.*[27]

Examples of the involvement of judgment throughout the creative process abound, even in activities designed to promote "lateral" thinking. One such activity which is very common in the educational world is that of brainstorming. Suppose a creative dance teacher is having the class "brainstorm" movements involving an autumn theme. De Bono would propose that all suggestions should be recorded without limitations imposed. However, students would not even make some suggestions. For instance, a student who suggests that the class move like crocodiles would be hard pressed to make a connection with the autumn theme. Thus, we make judgments even in this "lateral" thinking activity.

Perkins attempts to dissolve the dichotomy between creative thinking and ordinary thinking. He suggests that "these same resources [noticing, realizing, directed remembering, problem finding, critical reasoning, etc.] explain masterly and more ordinary creating. The master will notice more, remember more, exercise better critical judgment, and so on, but the processes involved are the same in kind."[28] Bailin emphasizes the non-necessity of extraordinary means for achieving extraordinary ends.

The studies of both Perkins and Weisberg support my conten-
tion that extraordinary means are not necessary in order to
achieve extraordinary ends, but that it is, rather, the skill with
which ordinary thinking processes are used and the purpose to
which they are put which enable outstanding results to be
achieved.[29]

The denial of a distinct creative process in favor of developing
skills necessary for enabling the creation of outstanding
results may, once again, not find favor with those advocating
free-expression. However, a closer examination of what is
really involved in being creative will demonstrate that the
creation of a product is the only way we can determine if a
so-called "creative" process is at work.

Creative Products

Recent philosophical work on the concept of creativity has
seen a shift in emphasis from viewing creativity in terms of
persons or processes, to viewing creativity in terms of the
creation of excellent *products*. Bailin emphasizes the need for
a creative product when, in discussing the relationship between creativity and product, she states that "certainly the
root meaning of the verb is connected with a product. To
create is to make or bring into being something which did not
exist previously, or at least not in that form. It would not make
sense to say that a person created if nothing is produced."[30]
To "bring something into being" results in something becoming available for public observation. White notes the distinction between a public product and a private process.

'Creative thinking', therefore, is not a peculiar type of thinking
that has different, non-publicly observable, features from other
types of thinking. A creative thinker is one whose thinking leads
to a result which conforms to criteria of value in one domain
or another. 'Creative' is a medal which we pin on public
products, not the name of private processes.[31]

Regarding creative thinking, Weisberg reiterates the notion
that "creative thinking becomes extraordinary because of

what the thinker *produces*, not because of the *way* in which the thinker produces it."[32]

If a condition necessary for a process to be deemed creative is the production of a product, we must elaborate what counts as a product. We typically consider creative products to exist in the domain of the arts. This is a fairly wide domain. ". . . 'work of art' hides an astonishing variety of products: a glass bottle, a sonnet, a symphony, an aria, a ballet, a novel."[33] Scientific inventions as well as theories could also fall under the rubric of creative products. Perkins suggests that "in real life, the outcome of a creative endeavor is almost always a complex product rather than a brief answer to a question . . . Theorems, theories, definitions, classification systems, arguments, analyses, field notes, interpretations, and evaluations are among many products of inquiry found in the study of the various disciplines."[34] Conceiving of theorems, analyses, etc., as products means that a product need not be something physical. This is true in the art world as well. A dance performance or a music concert, unlike a painting, is not physical in the sense that we can touch it. However, like a theorem or analysis, it is possible for an audience to perceive the dance performance or musical piece as a product. We can perceive a piece of choreography or music as a whole (comprised of a beginning, middle, end) which can be repeated by another group of dancers or musicians. So although a dance performance is not physical, it is something apart from the dancers which can be performed by someone else. This is not the case when a group of people get together, turn on some music and dance. Although this situation might build a sense of community and make people feel good about themselves, we should hesitate to say that a product was created. I am not denying the value of such activity, i.e., participation in such activity may be very therapeutic. However, we should not label such activity "creative."

One further distinction may be necessary at this point. When I suggest that a piece of music or choreography should be repeatable by another group of musicians or dancers, it may be helpful to make a type/token distinction. A piece of music or choreography could be considered a "type" while a particular performance could be considered a "token." This distinction makes it possible to refer to particular performances of improvisational jazz as creative products.

Although I have suggested that products are something apart from the person who produces them, we must still determine which products should be labelled "creative." A criterion which seems to be almost synonymous with the notion of creativity is that of originality. In examining the connection between originality and creativity, we must question the nature of the link between originality and novelty. Kneller states that any definition of creativity must include the essential element of novelty.[35] However, what does it mean to judge something as novel, and is novelty a sufficient condition for something to be deemed creative? Regarding the first question, Bailin notes that in identifying something as an innovation,

> *we must recognize in it a significant difference from what has come before. Something which is new is different in some way from that which is old or past ... The degree to which particular innovations depart from existing frameworks varies. Some creations may be new in some small way but remain, in most ways, much like other members of the same category, while others may differ quite radically. Nevertheless some type of connection to previous products does seem to be necessary for our recognition of difference and thus of novelty.[36]*

The idea that there is a connection between the "novel" product and previous products is reiterated by Abinun. Abinun questions the definition of the novel product as something that "did not exist before" meaning "has never previously been thought of by anyone who has ever lived."

> *This raises the question whether something like this is possible at all or, more importantly, how we can know about it, since we cannot examine the ideas of everyone that has ever existed. In addition, what about the same idea occurring independently to different persons, for example, to two or more scientists*

working in different parts of the world? . . . In a wider and
weaker sense, all human behaviors are unique. They are "new"
by virtue of being never duplicated or repeated precisely, not
even by the same individual. But surely, this is a very trivial
sense of "novelty," one that would designate almost everything
as new.[37]

Abinun's comment on the trivial sense of "novelty" leads
to a second question: is novelty a sufficient condition for
something to be deemed creative? Novelty should not be
viewed as a sufficient condition; a normative condition must
be involved. Bailin points out

the originality involved in creativity does not reduce to ar-
bitrary novelty. The fact that something is new is not a suffi-
cient condition for it to be deemed creative. It may not even be
a necessary condition, or at least not a primary consideration.
Some of the artistic masterpieces which we value highly today
are relatively non-divergent examples of the style which was
prevalent at the time, the works of Rembrandt or Gainsborough
for example. They are, however, outstanding examples of the
style and so expertly executed that they are still highly es-
teemed.[38]

Crittenden suggests that novelty is a necessary condition for
describing a work as creative but that "it cannot however be
treated as a sufficient condition. Mere novelty may only suc-
ceed in being bizarre or trivial. One has simply to recall those
cute inventions that frequently provide an amusing segment
of TV talk shows."[39] Clark suggests that "the word 'creative'
has both descriptive and evaluative functions . . . On the
whole, acts considered 'creative' in other contexts are not held
to be so when executed by those such as burglars or tax
evaders."[40] Thus, a product must have some value as well as
being original if it is to be considered "creative."

Creating Creative Products

If we accept that a product must be original and valuable in
order to be considered "creative," we must now examine how

a product achieves this standard. Contrary to the view discussed in the first section of this chapter, we must downplay the role of a mysterious source of inspiration. Rather, I would emphasize the employment of knowledge and skill in the creation of original and valuable products. To produce something original and valuable requires first, a knowledge of the tradition or discipline within which one is working; and secondly, skill and technique in the use of the materials with which one is working. Although it may appear paradoxical, we can recognize something as original, i.e., different from previous products, only if we have a thorough knowledge of these previous products in order to recognize the difference. Best notes the incoherence of the notion that the production of original products involves a radical break from the past.

> ... the aspiration to change everything, to make all things new, is incoherent. It is possible to move somewhere else only if one is already somewhere, and where one can move next depends on where one is now. The potential can be illustrated by analogy with the sailor who wants to restructure his ship in mid-ocean. Obviously he cannot abandon the ship to rebuild it from the beginning, since he needs the support of the main structure while he makes the changes. What changes he can make, and how quickly he can make them, depend on the character of the original. Nevertheless, progressively, he may be able to make considerable, even radical, alterations in the structure of the ship, while depending upon its support.[41]

Best also notes that "the methodological point that certain ways of teaching the disciplines of an activity can inhibit creativity should not be confused with the conceptual point that without a grasp of those disciplines, it would be impossible to be creative at all."[42] White makes a similar point regarding scientific creativity; "the mathematical or scientific understanding which this presupposes requires a rigorous initiation into these disciplines. Such imitation is not only helpful but necessary to the production of something valuable in these areas. This is a logical truth."[43]

Although artists and scientists may not utilize the term "logical truths," many explicitly express their debt to tradition. Abbs points out that "writers constantly assert that they have found their own 'voice' through the voices of others." He then proceeds to quote Virginia Woolf in her *Letter to a Poet*.

> *Think of yourself rather as something much humbler and less spectacular, but to my mind far more interesting – a poet in whom live all the poets of the past, from which all poets in time to come will spring. You have a touch of Chaucer in you, and something of Shakespeare, Dryden, Pope, Tennyson – to mention only the respectable among your ancestors – stir in your blood and sometimes move your pen a little to the right or to the left. In short you are an immensely ancient, complex, and continuous character.*[44]

This sentiment is echoed by Newton in his famous statement that "he has seen as far as he has only because he stood on the shoulders of giants."

The knowledge of the tradition or discipline within which one is working is also important in the developing of skills and technique necessary for producing valuable products. Regarding the technique necessary for work with a particular medium, Redfern makes the point that "to work within a certain medium is to do more than work with a set of materials; it is to employ those materials with some measure of how they have already been used for artistic purposes."[45] Having a knowledge of past technique is necessary for producing valuable products but it is also a prerequisite for creating something original. Regarding the skill necessary for creative achievement, Bailin notes that

> *this type of creative achievement presupposes skill – not simply low level skill applied mechanically, but rather higher order skill involving considerable judgment. The more skillful one is in terms of making high order judgments in the discipline, the greater will be the possibility that one will reach a point where one sees the necessity for and has the ability to make changes in the rules of the discipline itself.*[46]

Thus, knowledge *and* skills are necessary for creating products which are valuable and original and this is what it means when we refer to something as creative. Although we may view knowledge and skill as necessary for creating valuable products, they are not sufficient for creating something original. To create something original requires imaginative thinking, the topic of the next chapter.

Notes

[1] G. Dimondstein, *Exploring the Arts with Children* (New York: Mac-Millan Publishing Co., 1974), p. 167.

[2] R. Collingwood, *The Principles of Art* (Oxford: The Claredon Press, 1938), p. 29.

[3] Ibid., p. 129.

[4] V. Howard, *Artistry: The Work of Artists* (Indianapolis: Hackett Publishing Company, 1982), p. 118.

[5] J. Maitland, "Creativity," *Journal of Aesthetics and Art Criticism* 34 (Summer 1976): 397.

[6] Ibid., p. 398.

[7] P. Abbs, ed., *The Symbolic Order: A Contemporary Reader on the Arts Debate* (London: Falmer Press, 1989), p. 1.

[8] S. Bailin, *Achieving Extraordinary Ends: An Essay on Creativity* (Dordrecht: Kluwer Academic Publishers, 1988), p. 45.

[9] C. MacDonald, "Creative Dance in Elementary Schools: A Theoretical and Practical Justification," *Canadian Journal of Education* 16 (1991): 434.

[10] L. Wells, "Children on the Move," *Design* 80 (Sept. 1979): 18.

[11] J. Alter, "A Manifesto for Creative Dance in the Schools: Arts and Bodies are Basic," *Design* 85 (July/Aug. 1984): 28.

[12] L. Rubin, "Teaching Creative Dance," *Design* 80 (Sept. 1979): 28.

[13] A. Edry, "Dance for Non-Dancers," *Design* 85 (July/Aug. 1894): 38.

14 E. Wiseman, "Process – Not Product: Guidelines for Adding Creative Dance to the Elementary School Curriculum," *Journal of Physical Education and Recreation* 50 (1979): 47.

15 Bailin, *Achieving Extraordinary Ends*, p. 64.

16 Wiseman, "Process – Not Product," p. 47.

17 Plato, *Ion*, 543b.

18 Ibid., 543b.

19 Mozart, "A Letter," in P. Vernon, ed., *Creativity* (New York: Penguin Books Ltd., 1970), p. 55.

20 A. Koestler, *The Act of Creation* (London: Pan Books Ltd., 1964), p. 117.

21 Ibid., p. 117.

22 Tchaikovsky, "Letters," in P. Vernon, ed., *Creativity* (New York: Penguin Books Ltd., 1970), p. 57.

23 J. Maritain, "Creative Intuition in Art and Poetry," in A. Rothenberg and C. Hausman, eds., *The Creativity Question* (Durham, N. C.: Duke University Press, 1976), p. 105.

24 Koestler, *The Act of Creation*, p. 156.

25 J. White, "Creativity and Education: A Philosophical Analysis," *British Journal of Educational Studies* 16 (1969): 124.

26 R. Weisberg, *Creativity: Genius and Other Myths* (New York: W. H. Freeman and Co., 1986), p. 3.

27 Bailin, *Achieving Extraordinary Ends*, p. 67.

28 D. Perkins, *The Mind's Best Work* (Cambridge: Harvard University Press, 1981), p. 287.

29 Bailin, *Achieving Extraordinary Ends*, p. 76.

30 Ibid., p. 63.

31 White, *Creativity and Education*, p. 126.

32 Weisberg, *Creativity*, p. 69.

33 I. Winchester, "Creation and Creativity in Art and Science," *Interchange* 16 (1985): 74.

[34] D. Perkins, "Creativity by Design," *Educational Leadership* 42 (1984): 24.

[35] G. Kneller, *The Art and Science of Creativity* (New York: Holt, Rinehart and Winston, Inc., 1966), p. 3.

[36] Bailin, *Achieving Extraordinary Ends*, p. 8.

[37] J. Abinun, "Creativity and Education: Some Critical Remarks," *The Journal of Aesthetic Education* 15 (1981): 17-18.

[38] Bailin, *Achieving Extraordinary Ends*, p. 31.

[39] B. Crittenden, "Education and Creativity," in *Concepts in Education: Philosophical Studies* (Melbourne: A Mercy Teachers' College - 20th Century Publication, 1973), p. 33.

[40] W. Clark, "Some Thoughts on Teaching Creativity," *Journal of Aesthetic Education* 20 (1986): 21.

[41] D. Best, *Feeling and Reason in the Arts* (London: Allen & Unwin, 1985), p. 80.

[42] Ibid., p. 81.

[43] White, *Creativity and Education*, p. 135.

[44] Abbs, *The Symbolic Order*, p. 134.

[45] H. Redfern, *Questions in Aesthetic Education* (London: Allen & Unwin Publishers, 1986), p. 40.

[46] Bailin, *Achieving Extraordinary Ends*, p. 129.

Chapter V

The Imaginative Creation

The educational implications of the argument in the previous chapter make it incumbent upon creative dance teachers to help students acquire the knowledge and skill necessary to create original and valuable dance pieces in order to foster understanding through creative dance. However, knowledge and skill are not sufficient to create original dance pieces; students also require imaginative thinking. This suggestion requires that we examine what is meant by imaginative thinking, and how imagination is connected with understanding.

We refer to numerous educational activities as imaginative or valuable in helping develop the imagination of the students. However, it is not always clear what we mean by the imagination. Is the imagination a faculty of the mind? Do some people have "it" and others not? Is it something that can be developed? Or is having an imagination simply having the ability to conceive of ideas in a certain way? Is this ability context specific; that is, are people imaginative in one area of their lives but not another? Is it possible for there to be an imaginative person, i.e., a person having an imaginative ability that transcends all contexts? If having an imagination is an ability to conceptualize in a certain manner, can educators provide experiences which foster this ability? How does this ability differ from creative ability or the ability to fantasize? We must deal with these questions, among others, if we are to come to an understanding of what we mean by the concept of imagination. In order to understand how the term imagination has come to acquire the different meanings which have become associated with it, it would be fruitful to explicate how we have conceived of the concept historically.

Historical Conceptions

Since humanity began recording philosophical speculations, the term imagination has appeared in one form or another, occupying positions of varying degrees of importance. Beginning with Plato, philosophers have associated the imagination with sense or appearance. Plato considered the imagination to be concerned with image-making; an activity which expressed an appearance. He distinguished this activity from an expression of reality. According to Plato, the expression of appearances is a very inferior activity compared to the imitating of reality. He gives the example of a craftsman who imitates reality when he creates a particular couch (which is an imitation of the form or idea of a couch). The painter, on the other hand, imitates the imitation of the form of a couch. Thus, Plato refers to the painter as being "three removes from nature."[1] According to Plato, this distance from reality leaves the painter with little knowledge of that which he paints and he should not be taken seriously. Thus, the activity of the imagination is not held in high esteem by Plato.

Aristotle considered the imagination to be concerned with images, as did his teacher Plato. He considered the imagination to be something different from and yet connected to perception and thought. He went to great length to distinguish the imagination from sensation and opinion and the other faculties of knowledge and intellect. "Neither, again, can imagination be ranked with the faculties, like knowledge or intellect, which always judge truly: it may also be false."[2] For Aristotle, the imagination appeared to be at odds with the more esteemed faculties of the soul. "Because imaginations remain in us and resemble the corresponding sensations, animals perform many actions under their influence; some, that is, the brute, through not having intellect, and others, that is, men, because intellect is sometimes obscured by passion or disease or sleep."[3] Like Plato, Aristotle considered the imagination to be more of a disability than an activity or faculty whose development was to be encouraged. If Plato's and Aristotle's views on the imagination were representative of its position throughout Western thought, the story of the imagination would be short indeed. However, in the philosophical treatises proposed by Hume and Kant, the position occupied by the imagination became one of great importance.

Hume opened his *Treatise of Human Nature* with a discussion of the origin of ideas. According to Hume, the imagination's role is of utmost importance in the forming of complex ideas. "The idea of a substance as well as that of a mode, is nothing but a collection of simple ideas, that are united by the imagination, and have a particular name assigned them, by which we are able to recall, either to ourselves or others, that collection."[4] So unlike Plato and Aristotle, Hume held the activity of the imagination in high regard. Although Hume had great admiration for the activity of the imagination, he was unable to explicate any further how the imagination works. In fact, he referred to it as "a kind of magical faculty of the soul, which, [tho'] it be always most perfect in the greatest geniuses, and is properly what we call a genius, is however inexplicable by the utmost efforts of human understanding."[5]

A further attempt at understanding the activity of the imagination was made by Kant. According to Kant, "*Imagination* is the faculty of representing an object even without its presence in intuition."[6] For Kant, the imagination lay somewhere between the faculties of representation and understanding. In reference to the imagination, Kant states that

> . . . *because a certain form of sensuous intuition exists in the mind a priori which rests on the receptivity of the representative faculty (sensibility), the understanding, as a spontaneity, is able to determine the internal sense by means of the*

> *diversity of given representations, conformably to the syntheti-*
> *cal unity of apperception [consciousness] and thus to cogitate*
> *the synthetical unity of the apperception of the manifold of*
> *sensuous intuition a priori, as the condition to which must*
> *necessarily be submitted all objects of human intuition. And in*
> *this manner the categories as mere forms of thought receive*
> *objective reality* . . .[7]

Although Kant's description of the work of the imagination may not be easy to understand, one can grasp the fundamental importance of the imagination within Kant's metaphysical system. "It [the transcendental synthesis of the imagination] is an operation of the understanding on sensibility, and the first application of the understanding to objects of possible intuition, and at the same time the basis for the exercise of the other functions of that faculty."[8] Thus, not only does the imagination "make" objects out of sensations, it is the basis of one's ability to "recognize" objects. As Warnock so aptly put it:

> *Kant completed the account which Hume had begun of the part*
> *that imagination plays. Not only does it make objects out of*
> *some of the immediate but intermittent sensations which we*
> *experience, and induce us to say "same cat" of these, but it also*
> *induces us to apply object-words (that is, type-of-object-words)*
> *to our experiences, so that we can recognize a kind of ex-*
> *perience, and identify what we see as a cat.*[9]

According to Sartre, however, the great metaphysicians of the seventeenth and eighteenth century erred by confusing imagining and perceiving. This confusion was based upon what Sartre referred to as "the naïve metaphysics of the image."[10] In order to understand how this naïve metaphysics arose, Sartre distinguished between essential sameness and existential identity. Sartre illustrated this distinction by refer- ring to a sheet of paper on his desk. When Sartre turned his head away from the desk and looked at the wall, he no longer saw the sheet of paper. "I know perfectly well, however, that it has not annihilated itself; it is prevented by its inertness. It has just ceased to be *for me.*"[11] Still looking at the wall, Sartre was able to "see" the sheet of paper again. Sartre noted that existence in the form of image is a mode of being which is difficult to grasp since one is in the habit of conceiving all modes of existence as physical.

Consequently, as soon as one shifts from pure contemplation of the image as such to thinking about images without forming them, one slides from essential identity of image and object to an alleged existential identity. Since the image, in this case, is the object, one draws the conclusion that the image exists in the same fashion as the object.[12]

According to Sartre, there are three types of consciousness by which the same object can be given to us: "to perceive, conceive, imagine."[13] Regarding the imagination, Sartre noted its resemblance to perception. "Let us note first that it seems to belong to perception. In the one, as in the other, the object presents itself in profiles, in projections . . . Only we no longer have to make a tour of it: the cube as an image is presented immediately for what it is."[14] Thus, the distinction between imagining and perceiving lies in the potential for the immediate knowledge of an image. "The image teaches nothing: it is organized exactly like the objects which do produce knowledge, but it is complete at the very moment of its appearance."[15] Thus, according to Sartre, imagining is a type of consciousness, albeit inferior to the other types, i.e., perceiving and conceiving.

With Sartre, there was a move from referring to a faculty of the imagination to referring to the process of imagining. This move is epitomized in the work of Ryle. Where Sartre reflected upon images in order to determine their distinctive characteristics, Ryle set out to show that when people are seeing things in their minds' eyes and hearing things in their heads, this is no proof that there exist things which they see and hear, or that the people are seeing or hearing anything. Although Sartre and Ryle differ in their methods of inquiry, they seem to reach the same conclusion; that although imaging occurs, images are not *seen*. In answering the question "how can a person seem to hear a tune, when there is no tune to be heard?," Ryle's response is reminiscent of Sartre's reflections.

We already know, and have known since childhood, in what situations to describe people as imagining that they see or hear or do things. The problem, so far as it is one, is to construe these descriptions without falling back into the idioms in which we talk of seeing horse-races, hearing concerts and committing murders. It is into these idioms that we fall back the moment we say that to fancy one sees a dragon is to see a real dragon-phantasm, or that to pretend to commit murder is to commit a real mock-murder, or that to seem to hear a tune is to hear a real mental tune.[16]

In illuminating the problem of images as he does, Ryle hoped to show that hearing a tune one does not really "hear" is simply a question about the concept of imagining. In elaborating on the concept of imagining, Ryle pointed out that

there are hosts of widely divergent sorts of behaviour in the conduct of which we should ordinarily and correctly be described as imaginative. The mendacious witness in the witness-box, the inventor thinking out a new machine, the constructor of a romance novel, the child playing bears, and Henry Irving are all exercising their imaginations; but so, too, are the judge listening to the lies of the witness, the colleague giving his opinion of the new invention, the novel reader, the nurse who refrains from admonishing the 'bears' for their subhuman noises, the dramatic critic and the theatre-goers.[17]

Having described certain sorts of behavior as imaginative, Ryle concluded that there is no special faculty of imagination.

With no role for a faculty of imagination to fill, the concept of the imagination seemed to have taken on a new meaning and a less fundamental role than that accorded to it by Hume and Kant. To elaborate on this "new" meaning, it is fruitful to consider the work of Robin Barrow, who adopts Ryle's thesis in his formulation of the concept of imagination. Barrow, like Ryle, denies the existence of the imagination as an entity.

According to Barrow, "to be imaginative is to have the inclination and ability consciously to conceive of the unusual and effective in particular contexts."[18] In explicating Barrow's concept of imagination, it is important to understand what he means by unusual, effective, conceive, and particular contexts. Barrow suggests that the criterion of unusualness means seeing beyond the obvious and immediately apparent. Regarding the criterion of effectiveness, Barrow argues that something is effective if it is conducive to a good solution to the problem at hand. An imaginative salesperson has to come up with techniques that are not merely unusual but that also sell products. In espousing the unusual and the effective as criteria for imaginative conceptualizations, Barrow points out that both criteria must be met.

> *Merely to generate unusual ideas does not deserve the epithet* imaginative, *for if the ideas are absurd, unworkable, logically incoherent, and so forth, then no normative label is deserved at all. Besides, we have other words to label the mere generation of unusual ideas such as* bizarre, prolific, *or* inventive, *(depending on precisely what we want to imply), which do not suggest anything about their quality. Conversely, the generation of merely effective ideas does not constitute imagination, but is what we would label "competent," "sound," or "good."*[19]

According to Barrow, imaginative activity involves conceptualization; that is, an understanding of something is involved. He suggests that an imaginative road sweeper or an imaginative auto mechanic would seem an incongruous idea since sweeping roads or fixing cars does not produce conceptualizations. Finally, one must understand what Barrow means when he speaks of particular contexts in reference to unusual and effective conceptualizations. "'This is an unusual and effective implement' makes no sense if there is no answer to the question 'for what?'"[20] Thus it is logically possible to have an imaginative person, i.e., someone having an ability to conceptualize imaginatively in all contexts, but this would be a rare occurrence.

The Imaginative Versus the Imagination

What are we to make of this historical account of conceptions of the imagination? Which, if any, is the correct one? Any proposed conception would have to take into account the fundamental differences between the imagination, imagining and the imaginative. Plato, Aristotle, Hume and Kant all conceived of the imagination as a faculty of the mind. In Plato's and Aristotle's account, the use of this faculty involved imagining. They conceived of imagining as involving image-making; thus, it was closely associated with the faculty of perception. Hume's and Kant's faculty of the imagination was more closely associated with the faculty of conception; a place where ideas were united. I will examine the issue of whether imagining involves perceiving or conceiving in a later section. At this point I will argue in favor of the conception of the imaginative, rather than thinking in terms of a faculty of the imagination.

Whether there is something called an imagination as opposed to something being imaginative is reminiscent of the argument regarding creative products in chapter four. Just as creative persons can only be judged to be creative by their products, likewise persons with a well-developed imagination can only be judged to have such a capacity as a result of their conceptions or perceptions. We cannot observe a faculty of the mind, only what results from its use. Thus, Sartre, Ryle and Barrow propose more accurate accounts of the imaginative as opposed to those advocating the existence of a faculty of the imagination. Barrow's account would seem to supersede the other accounts since Sartre's conception of the imaginative as a type of consciousness and Ryle's conception of imaginative kinds of behaviour would seem to involve conceptualizing. Whether Barrow's criterion of what makes a conceptualization imaginative is sufficient is the topic of the next section.

A Premature Dismissal of Imagining?

Although I am suggesting that Barrow's conception of the imaginative is correct, there seems to be an aspect of imagining which has been left out in his account. As Casey notes, "Imagination as a fixed faculty is indeed dead, eviscerated in the 'objective' accounts of many modern thinkers. But imagining is very much alive, its potency as an act manifesting itself in daily feats of fancy as well as in the production of poets."[22] In suggesting that there is something more to imagination than conceptualizing unusually and effectively, I must emphasize that I am *not* advocating a return to the pre-Rylean notion of a faculty of imagination. An alternative account would be White's contention that "to imagine something is to *think of* it as possibly being so."[23] In other words, imagination "is a thought of the possible rather than of the actual, of what might or could be so rather than of what is or must be so, even when what is possible happens, unknown to the thinker, to be actual."[24] Thus, having an imagination is nothing more than thinking but it involves thinking about something in a particular way. Herein lies the difference between Barrow's imaginative conceptualizing and White's imagining. Barrow is focusing on a product, a certain type of conceptualization, i.e., one which is unusual and effective. White is focusing on a process; a way of thinking about something, i.e., as if that something (it could be anything) is possibly so. It must be emphasized that Barrow's imaginative product and White's imaginative process are not dichotomous. However, it is possible to imagine in the sense advocated by White, without necessarily producing a product, i.e., a certain conceptualization. This would be the case when children are imagining that they are bunny rabbits. Although they are thinking of themselves as bunnies, they have not produced some unusual and effective conceptualization. It may be unusual to think of oneself as a bunny (especially in the case of an adult), but one could not really label oneself as conceptualizing effectively when imagining that one is a bunny.

Thus, Barrow and White are considering two different senses of "imagination." Furthermore, Barrow's conception of imaginative products may be subsumed under the rubric of creative. In chapter four, I suggested that the criterion for something to be deemed creative was the creation of an original and valuable product. We may view a conceptualization as a product. Perkins emphasizes this contention when he states that

> *in real life, the outcome of a creative endeavor is almost always a complex product rather than a brief answer to a question . . . Theorems, theories, definitions, classification systems, arguments, analyses, field notes, interpretations, and evaluations are among many products of inquiry found in the study of the various disciplines.*[25]

If we view a conceptualization as a product of inquiry, then having an unusual and effective conceptualization would not be unlike producing an original and valuable product. Thus, Barrow's conception of imaginative is no different than the conception of creative I argued for in chapter four.

Although Barrow's conception of imaginative may be referred to as creative, this is not the case with White's conception of imaginative thinking. As mentioned previously, imagining oneself to be a bunny does not result in the creation of an original and valuable product. However, this sense of imagining is related to, and important for, creating original and valuable products, which is important for fostering understanding. I will make this connection in chapter six, but at this point I must expand upon what it means "to think of something as possibly being so".

Perceiving or Conceiving As?

White suggests that much of the work done in the area of the imagination has involved a mistaken assimilation of imagination and visualization. It is tempting to suggest that the common thread running through the different senses of imagination is the Wittgensteinian notion of "seeing as." Recall Wittgenstein's duck-rabbit illustration; the picture can be "seen as" a rabbit's head or "seen as" a duck's head. This explanation may account for examples such as students in a dance class being directed to imagine that colorful scarves are leaves blowing in the wind. Thus, the scarves could be "seen as" scarves or they could be "seen as" blowing leaves.

However, a cursory look at the different senses of imagining or imaginative reveals the inability of a function of perception to adequately account for all potential senses of imagination. Redfern suggests that, although neither complete nor exclusive, it appears possible to draw five major distinctions when referring to the concept of imagining. These distinctions are:

1) *Imaging – the occurrence of mental imagery.*

Two types:
a) undirected – e.g., daydreaming;
b) directed – either self-directed or guided from the outside, e.g., a teacher asking students to conjure up an image of some sort or other.

2) *Empathizing – appreciating in some measure how a person appraises and therefore feels about a situation.*

3) *Believing falsely – with children it is often the case that they take the imaginary for the real as a result of acting; make-believe passes into belief.*

4) *Acting – playing a part or pretending.*

5) *Using "creative imagination" – seeing things in a way different from how they actually or already are in order to produce public artifacts and performances judged to be of excellence according to the standards characteristic of the particular activity or discipline in question.*[26]

Scruton, in his discussion of the various phenomena grouped under the heading of the imagination, wants to account for the following:

forming an image ('picturing'); imagining in its various forms (imagining that . . . , imagining what it would be like if . . . , imagining what it is like to. . . . : some of these constructions are propositional, some not; some relate to knowledge that . . . some to knowledge by acquaintance); doing something with imagination, (imagination as adverbial rather than predictive); using imagination to see something; seeing an aspect.[27]

Although Redfern's reference to "imaging" and Scruton's "forming an image" can easily be viewed as a function of "seeing as," it is not so obvious that "empathizing" or "imagining what it would be like if . . ." involve perception. Thus, the notion of "seeing as" cannot account for all potential senses of imagination. As Egan notes, "by recognizing that our everyday use of 'imagination' refers, perhaps most often, to the non-pictorial and non-imageable, we realize that the imagination is not simply a capacity to form images, but is a capacity to think in a particular way."[28] Hence, we come back to White's notion that imagining involves our capacity to *think* of the possible rather than just the actual.

The suggestion that "seeing as" is a component of all senses of imagination is a result of a conflation between perceiving and conceiving. Having suggested that the potential senses of imagination do not all entail "perceiving as," it may be fruitful to consider whether they all entail "conceiving as." Redfern's sense of empathizing is a case of Scruton's "imagining what it would be like to . . .;" in this case, imagining what it would be like to be the person with whom you are empathizing. This would seem to be a situation where the person empathizing is thinking of something as possibly being so, i.e., being "in the shoes" of the other person. Redfern's senses of acting and believing falsely (which is a result of acting to the point of not being able to separate the make-believe from reality) are synonymous with Scruton's "imagining that . . ." and "imagining what it is like to . . . ." These situations are obviously a case of thinking of something as possibly being so. The actor playing MacBeth is thinking of himself as MacBeth and his fellow actors as King Duncan, Lady MacBeth, etc. The child who is "believing falsely" in an imaginary friend is thinking of his/her imaginary friend as possibly being so (being real, that is).

Although the above senses of the imaginative would seem to involve "conceiving as" or "thinking of something as possibly being so," it does not seem to be as obvious that "imaging," "using imagination to see something," and "seeing an aspect" involve "conceiving as." However, forming an image is simply thinking of something as possibly being so in a visual sense. Whatever is being imaged may exist in reality but it need not. Thus, if you are imagining your bedroom, you are thinking of something in a visual sense which actually exists. On the other hand, if you are forming an image of a dance you would like to create, you are thinking of how the dancers would move "in your head" without the dance actually existing at that point. In using your imagination to see something, i.e., to see a cloud as the shape of an elephant, you are thinking about what an elephant looks like and thinking of the cloud as possibly being so (that is, the shape of an elephant). Seeing an aspect is obviously a function of perception, but not to the exclusion of conception. In seeing Wittgenstein's duck-rabbit figure as a duck, one is seeing a figure drawn on paper, but one is also thinking of the figure as possibly being so (that is, a duck). If a Gestalt shift is achieved and one sees the figure as a rabbit, the same figure is still being seen but the observer is thinking of it as possibly being a rabbit. Thus, thinking is of fundamental importance in the situation of "seeing as." This point is reiterated by Winchester when he suggests that "'seeing as' is not part of perception – it is related to imaging and the imagination: prior knowledge, prior acquaintance, or mastery of a technique, or sometimes mere social place, are preliminary to the possibility of an aspect."[29] Although one can think without images, one cannot image without thinking. As mentioned previously, having an imagination is simply thinking, but thinking in a particular way, that is, thinking of something as possibly being so.

Thinking of something as possibly being so is directly related to interpretive reasoning which, as discussed in chapter three, is integral to attaining understanding through the arts. We can attain a unique understanding of human experience by apprehending the aesthetic features which make the expression of the content of the work unique. However, in apprehending these aesthetic features, we must utilize imaginative thinking; that is, thinking of these aesthetic features as possibly being so – as possibly expressing something. In appreciating the dance piece *Balance*, cited in chapter three, we must "conceive of" the way the dancer reaches, balances precariously and then falls as possibly expressing humankind's desire for balance in their lives and the difficulty involved in achieving it. Thus, in appreciating works of art, imaginative thinking is fundamental to interpretive reasoning and this reasoning is fundamental to attaining the rich understanding which is possible through experience with the arts.

A Fluency Problem?

White also defines the imaginative person as "one with the ability to think of lots of possibilities, usually with some richness of detail."[30] Although his conception of the imagination as thinking of possibilities appears to be correct, a caveat is in order regarding the notion of thinking of *lots* of possibilities. Bailin addresses this problem when she discusses the generative versus the evaluative aspects of thinking. Her thesis is that imaginative thinking does not only involve the generating of possibilities, but also involves an evaluative component. "The main point of the account, however, is that the free play of ideas is never really totally free, that there are constraints on what ideas are generated, that evaluation and criticism are very much aspects of imaginative invention."[31] A prime example of an activity which is typically considered to be purely generative in nature is brainstorming. Teachers are cautioned when utilizing this approach to guard against prejudgment, i.e., ". . . students should be given the time and freedom to let their imaginations go, to brainstorm. It is especially important to guard against prejudgment and premature closure, since the best ideas sometimes come late, and prejudgment can block the kind of open exploration that can yield these ideas."[32] However, judgment *is* involved in this generation of ideas. For instance, if a class was brainstorming for ideas for a dance piece having to do with the different seasons, the students would not suggest the idea of a toaster.

Students do not generate just any ideas in brainstorming, only those ideas which respond to the constraints of the situation.

Thus, it is not the quantity of ideas solicited but rather the quality which characterizes the imaginative. Quality requires, as Winchester pointed out, prior knowledge, prior acquaintance or mastery of a technique. The contention that knowledge is necessary for imaginative thinking is emphasized by Egan. "We can only construct possible worlds, can only think of things as possibly being so, out of what we already know."[33] Prior knowledge is necessary if we are to make sound judgments and, again citing Winchester, "imagination is central to judgment."[34] The relationship between imagination and judgment will be explored in the following chapter. At this point, the conception of the imagination I am advocating merits restatement; imagining is thinking of something as being possibly so and the imaginative person is someone who thinks of "quality" possibilities. These "quality" possibilities are reminiscent of Barrow's "effective" conceptualizations. However, unlike Barrow's "conceptualizations," which seem limited to a "product" situation, the conception of imagination as thinking of something as being possibly so accounts for "imaginative" activity which may not lead directly to the creation of a product, e.g., hopping like bunnies. Much of the activity which takes place in the creative dance class is of this nature, that is, imaginative as opposed to creative. The relationship between the imaginative and the creative and implications for creative dance education will be examined in the following chapter.

Notes

1 Plato, *The Republic*, Book X 597.

2 Aristotle, *De Anima*, III 427b27 - 428a21.

3 Ibid., 428b18 - 429a9.

4 D. Hume, *A Treatise of Human Nature*, ed. L. A. Selby-Bigge, 2nd ed. (London: Oxford University Press, 1978, first published 1888), p. 16.

5 Ibid., p. 24.

6 I. Kant, *Critique of Pure Reason*, trans. J. M. D. Meiklejohn (London: J. M. Dent & Sons, Ltd., 1984, first published 1781), book i, chapter ii, section ii, p. 104.

7 Ibid., p. 104.

8 Ibid.

9 M. Warnock, *Imagination* (London: Faber and Faber, 1976), p. 28.

10 J. P. Sartre, *Imagination: A Psychological Critique*, trans. Forrest William (Ann Arbor: The University of Michigan Press, 1962), p. 6.

11 Ibid., pp. 2-3.

12 Ibid., p. 6.

13 J. P. Sartre, *The Psychology of Imagination*, trans. Bernard Frechtman (New York: Washington Square Press, Inc., 1966), p. 8.

14 Ibid., pp. 9-10.

15 Ibid., p. 10.

16 G. Ryle, *The Concept of Mind* (New York: Barnes & Noble, Inc., 1949), p. 251.

17 Ibid., p. 256.

18 R. Barrow, "Some Observations on the Concept of Imagination" in K. Egan & D. Nadaner, eds., *Imagination and Education* (New York: Teachers College Press, 1988), p. 84.

19 Ibid., p. 84.

20 Ibid., p. 86.

21 Ryle, *Concept of Mind*, pp. 257-258.

22 E. Casey, *Imagining: A Phenomenological Study* (Bloomington, Indiana: Indiana University Press, 1976), p. 3.

23 A. White, *The Language of Imagination* (Oxford: Basil Blackwell, 1990), p. 184.

24 Ibid., p. 186.

25 D. Perkins, "Creativity by Design," *Educational Leadership* 42 (1984): 24.

26 H. Redfern, *Concepts in Modern Educational Dance* (London: Henry Kimpton Publishers, 1973), pp. 6-16.

27 R. Scruton, *Art and Imagination: A Study of the Philosophy of Mind* (London: Metheun & Co. Ltd., 1974), pp. 91-92.

28 K. Egan, *Imagination in Teaching and Learning: The Middle School Years* (London, Ontario: The Althouse Press, 1992), p. 4.

29 I. Winchester, *Notes on Aesthetics* (unpublished manuscript, February 10, 1978), p. 29.

30 White, *The Language of Imagination*, p. 185.

31 S. Bailin, *Achieving Extraordinary Ends: An Essay of Creativity* (Dordrecht: Kluwer Academic Publishers, 1988), p. 121.

32 *Biology: The Study of Life* (Allyn & Bacon, 1987), High-School Biology Textbook, p. CCT-18.

33 Egan, *Imagination in Teaching and Learning*, p. 52.

34 Winchester, *Notes on Aesthetics*, p. 42.

Chapter VI

Implications for Creative Dance Education

Fostering understanding through creative dance involves the appreciation and creation of new and valuable products. This conception of creative dance education runs counter to what typically occurs in the creative dance class, e.g., children continuously engaged in "free expression" activities. Such activities may be valuable, i.e., self-expression as therapeutic, exploration of materials as necessary *beginning* steps to creating aesthetically valuable products, etc., but we should clarify their objectives and elucidate their relationship to creating aesthetically valuable dances. I will now attempt to clarify the objectives of activities done in the name of creative dance and to elucidate the relationship between these activities and the appreciation and creation of new and valuable products.

As I discussed in chapter one, creative dance is often viewed as a therapeutic "process." Wiseman suggests that "there will be some who wish to develop expressive movement into an art form, and these children will need skilled teachers, discipline, technique and the experience of communicating through dance to observers, but I wish to talk about the process of dancing and not the product."[1] This proposed dichotomy between process and product should be reconsidered since, if creative dance is expressive in nature, it would seem that its purpose would best be fulfilled if the expression was recognizable by observers. Furthermore, as Bailin points out, "if expression must necessarily be in a medium, then control of the medium is a prerequisite for expression."[2] Since the medium of creative dance is the dancer's body, the dancer must become familiar with how it moves. This requires knowledge of, and skill in utilizing, the basic movement elements.

Contrary to Wiseman's inference that creative dance teachers need not be skilled, creative dance teachers must have a theoretical and practical knowledge of basic movement elements. Unlike dance forms such as ballet, a workable knowledge of basic movement elements need not take a lifetime to acquire. Acquiring a basic movement vocabulary is possible by studying movement analyses, such as the one proposed by Laban. Examples of Laban's movement elements include "body awareness, space awareness, the awareness of weight, time, and flow; and the adaptation to partners and groups."[3] Dance theoreticians have written numerous handbooks suggesting lessons based on themes developed from these movement elements.[4] Although these handbooks provide many good lesson ideas, there appears to be a dearth of writing regarding the development of these movement themes to the point where a valuable product can be created, i.e., an aesthetically valuable piece of choreography. What is required is additional training in the area of aesthetics, particularly the acquisition of the body of knowledge involving aesthetic features. Acquiring a basic movement vocabulary as well as an "aesthetic features" vocabulary should be possible within the time constraints of teacher training programs.

To explain this lack of consideration of a product resulting from the development of movement elements, it would seem critical to consider the age of the students involved in creative dance. Typically, creative dance is taught in the primary grades. By the intermediate grades, creative dance experiences are often replaced by folk dance, and by the senior years, dance is often relegated to electives in social and/or jazz dance.[5] A partial explanation may be that teachers perceive creative dance as the acquisition of basic motor skills rather than as an art form. For example, if creative dance is perceived as an activity to learn the basic motor skill of hopping, once the six year old has learned how to hop, the teacher may not see the need to continue creative dance activities focusing on hopping. However, if creative dance is perceived as an expressive art form, there would be no age limit to the use of hopping to express ideas and feelings, i.e., the feeling of instability, etc.

By implying that creative dance should be taught beyond the primary grades, I am not suggesting that the activities performed in creative dance class should be the same throughout the educational curriculum. In the primary grades there may be more of a focus on the development of basic motor skills, because students must develop these skills before they can use them for expressive purposes. However, a focus on the development of motor skills does not preclude the creation of original and valuable products. If children are to participate in creative dance which is truly creative, they must, from an early age, see that the skills they are learning can be used to create "dances." These dances will not be of the same calibre as those created in the later grades, but even the creation of a simple sequence (with a beginning, a middle and an end) which can be repeated will reinforce the importance of a product. The quality of the product will increase as students learn to use their bodies in a more expressive manner.

The suggestion that students must learn basic motor skills before they can use them for expressive purposes does not mean that, in the primary grades, creative dance is used to learn motor skills and only in the later grades do students use these skills to express ideas and feelings. One of Laban's movement categories includes the awareness of weight, time and flow. Thus children can learn to move with different weight, i.e., light or heavy; in different time, i.e., slow or fast; or with varying flow, i.e., bound or free. Young children can experience these different effort qualities while walking. They need not have mastered hopping or galloping to experience what it means to stomp or flit lightly around the room. As children gain experience with these effort qualities, they can be used in more complex combinations. Laban isolates eight basic effort actions which are constitutive of different combinations of weight, time and flow: 1) Pressing – firm, sustained, direct; 2) Flicking – light, sudden, flexible; 3) Punching or Thrusting – firm, sudden, direct; 4) Floating or Flying – light, sustained, flexible; 5) Wringing – firm, sustained, flexible; 6) Dabbing – light, sudden, direct; 7) Slashing – firm, sudden, flexible; 8) Gliding – light, sustained, direct.[6] These eight basic effort actions may be too complicated for the primary student, but they can form the basis of numerous lessons for the older student. In summary, teaching basic effort actions to the primary student and more complex effort actions to the older student will help students develop the ability to use movement in an expressive manner. The ability to use movement in an expressive manner is integral to the creation of aesthetically valuable products (i.e., works with aesthetic features) and are important for fostering understanding through creative dance.

Having discussed the conception of creative dance leading to the creation of aesthetically valuable products, we must now consider the implications of this conception for the *methods* of teaching creative dance. Contrary to much of the thinking today regarding creativity in education, teachers can initially develop the knowledge and skill of their students through imitation. Thus, there is a fundamental connection between appreciating and creating valuable works of art. I must emphasize that the term "imitation" does not necessarily mean mere copying. Rather, I refer to the Renaissance concept of "imitation," which Bantock points out

> *involved the internalization of aspects of past achievements, an essential element in creativity. We use this word 'creativity' carelessly and sometimes – though today perhaps less than we used to do – we seem to think that any manifestation of child behaviour if it's on paper somehow constitutes a manifestation of the creative. But, as our philosophers have pointed out, the essential element in the concept of creativity is some element of value; and therefore the Renaissance concept of 'imitation',*

with its notion of the internalization of past models as essential elements in the creative process, seems to be a very fruitful one.[7]

The Renaissance notion of imitation is evident in the following description by the Afro-Carribbean poet Derek Walcott, who was encouraged by two teachers and a library: "It couldn't afford trash. I've often wondered what would have happened if I hadn't encountered Shakespeare, Dickens – all those Faber and Dent library books – and the poets. *I would set out to imitate them*: I'd do one like Auden, another like Dylan Thomas – it was an apprenticeship" [italics added].[8] Abbs emphasizes that "Walcott's notion of 'a guild of poets, a craft in the best sense' practiced expresses a sense of apprenticeship, of emulation, of continuity and development in art-making which is necessary to any arts education, whatever the art-form and whatever the age of the student."[9] Abbs notes that this sort of imitation of inspirational models is necessary "whatever the age of the student." Gardner, who proposes a developmental analysis of artistic competence, stresses that middle childhood is "a time when the child is especially open and undefensive and is receptive to aid, suggestion and *inspirational models*" [italics added].[10]

The "inspirational models" teachers present to students need not only be historical. The teacher him/herself is a primary model and possible source of inspiration. This is evident in Stockhausen's approach to teaching music: "If such a person spends several weeks, several months, with me, he begins to discover things. He'll discover the same as me."[11] Regarding the teaching of creative dance, Ritson presents a five stage model, where the second level involves imitating.

Practice at imitating is second in the learning process toward creative dance. It helps create a positive attitude toward participation and allows children to grasp definitions of movement variables, review skills and concepts, and take advantage of modeling opportunities. Imitating is provided so the children may move easily and freely. Clearly, children can learn by modeling other's behaviors.[12]

Note that in Ritson's model, imitating is an early stage in the teaching of creative dance. I must emphasize that the student must not stop at imitating the teacher or other "inspirational models." Rather, imitation is an important means of acquiring knowledge and skills which students can use to begin creating dance pieces of a more original nature. The quality of these pieces will develop as the depth of knowledge and degree of skill increases.

The suggestion that an important method of teaching creative dance is through imitation not only runs counter to what typically occurs in the creative dance class, but it also reinforces the need for the teacher to be well versed in the skills and techniques required in creating valuable products. The teacher may not be an accomplished artist per se, but a knowledge of the tradition is necessary to fully appreciate excellent work and an appreciation of such work is a prerequisite for attempting the creation of works of value. Advocating the creation of valuable works does not mean that the teacher withdraw recognition of a child's product until it is of "Nureyev calibre." Rather, a teacher can praise a product at different stages. What is important, however, is that the child is working toward the creation of an aesthetically valuable product.

The appreciation and creation of aesthetically valuable products require two things: skills/knowledge and imaginative thinking. We require skills and knowledge to appreciate and create something of value. We require imaginative thinking to think of something original, i.e., to think of something that we have not thought of before as possibly being so. Thus, imaginative thinking is necessary to appreciate and create *original* products, and skills and knowledge are necessary to appreciate and create *valuable* products. The role of the imaginative and the creative, and the interplay between the two, would benefit from a more detailed examination.

The Role of the Imaginative

In chapter five, I suggested that being imaginative involved thinking of possibilities or thinking of something as possibly being so. This is a critical element in both the creation and appreciation of creative dance. In conceiving a potential creative dance piece, it is essential that the choreographer (this term will be used to designate anyone creating a dance piece – regardless of level achieved) arrive at the best possible means of conveying what he/she conceives. This requires thinking of a variety of possible means of expressing what he/she wishes to express. Thinking of a variety of possibilities will be referred to as the first sense of imaginative thinking. If the choreographer has "hit upon" a *valuable* means of expression immediately, without an exploration of numerous possibilities, then he/she may still have to think of this means of expressing as possibly being so (the second sense of imaginative thinking).

For example, if a choreographer wishes to create a dance conveying the image of a snowstorm, he/she may immediately think of having the dancers whirl and twirl their bodies at different levels with a growing intensity. If these movements create an effective image, he/she will not have to think of other possibilities. However, he/she would still be thinking imaginatively in the second sense if the whirling, twirling dancers were thought of as possibly being blowing snow. Anytime throughout the creative process, the choreographer may think of another possibility, e.g., the "bunching" together of dancers to show an increase in the "thickness" of the snowstorm, and thus, the first sense of imaginative thinking can recur throughout the creative activity. The second sense of imaginative thinking must be present at all times if the choreographer is to create a believable portrayal of a snowstorm.

Both senses of imaginative thinking may be involved in the appreciation of creative dance. For example, if an audience is experiencing a dance where dancers are moving very slowly to very somber music and then one dancer seems to "buck the flow" and speed up his/her movements, the audience may think of different possible interpretations. One interpretation may be that the choreographer is making a statement regarding non-conformity. Another possibility may involve a less literal interpretation. It may be that the audience simply experiences the dissonance involved in watching fast movements to slow music. The first possibility would seem to require imaginative thinking in the second sense but this may not be the case with the second interpretation. The first interpretation would involve thinking of the fast-moving dancer as possibly being a non-conformist. Such thinking as possibly being so does not seem to play a significant role in the second interpretation. Thus *both* senses of imaginative thinking need *not* be present in the appreciation of creative dance but at least one sense of imaginative thinking is always present in the creation and appreciation of an aesthetic activity.

Sheppard emphasizes the important role played by the imagination in appreciating art. The conception of the imagination as the thinking of possibilities or of something as possibly being so is important for appreciating both representational and expressionist art.

> *When we respond to A as a representation of B, we are not simply deciphering a code or recognizing a resemblance. Our imagination links A and B together, guided by whatever cues the artist has included in the work. We value representational art which gives scope to this capacity of the imagination [A as possibly being B]. The art of trompe-l'oeil is not valued highly precisely because it is so easy to take the picture for the reality. There is little room here to exercise the imagination and no opportunity for the mental balancing act involved in seeing a picture both as a representation of something else and as a configuration of shapes and colours.*[13]

In expressionist art, the artist is often attempting to express an emotion or feeling. For the audience to understand what is being expressed, they will have to use their imagination, i.e., thinking of a feeling or emotion as possibly being so. This will often require them to think of situations where they have felt the feeling or emotion being expressed by the artist. In a sense, the audience recreates the experience which stimulates that feeling or emotion. Sheppard alludes to this process when she suggests that "to grasp the happiness I am expressing by my singing and dancing others must attend to what I am doing and use their imaginations to recreate my experience for themselves."[14] Recreating a feeling or emotion distinguishes aesthetic imagining from fantasizing or daydreaming. "When we daydream, when we conjure up scenes and people in our own minds and imagine our reactions to them, we imagine feeling emotions but this is different from the imagining involved in aesthetic experience. Daydreaming is free to wander at will as the response to a work of art is not."[15] The features of a work of art, i.e., aesthetic features, what is represented, and often the title, place some constraints on what we imagine or what we think of as possibly being so.

As I suggested in chapter five, one can attain a unique understanding of the human experience by apprehending the aesthetic features which make the expression of the content of the work unique. Apprehending these aesthetic features involves imaginative thinking; that is, thinking of these aesthetic features as possibly being so — as possibly expressing something. In creating works of art, deciding upon how to express something also requires thinking of aesthetic features as expressing possibilities. Thus, imaginative thinking plays a fundamental role in both appreciating and creating works of art and this imaginative thinking, combined with the feelings evoked through the apprehension of aesthetic features, is fundamental to attaining the rich understanding which is possible through experience with the arts.

The Role of the Creative

If skill and knowledge are required to create something of value, while imaginative thinking is required to think of something original, it may appear that a dichotomy has been set up between the two. However, this is not the case. In fact, there is a constant interplay between the use of skills and knowledge and using them in imaginative ways, i.e., thinking of something as possibly being so and using skill and knowledge to portray this image. Bailin notes the existence of this interplay when she suggests that imagination

> *is not an element which is separable from skill and which transcends it. Rather, they are closely interconnected, with imagination manifested in the execution of skill and skill involved in the development of an imaginative vision. Skills are suffused with imagination, as is, in fact, our thinking in general. All intelligent thought and behaviour involves going beyond the given and has an imaginative, generative component which is constrained by skill and judgment. This interplay of skill and imagination is central to the growth of traditions and thus to how creative achievement is possible.*[16]

Bailin proceeds to give examples from different art forms demonstrating the interplay between imagination and skill. Regarding music, she suggests that "there are always numerous judgments to be made regarding such features as rhythm, tempo, and phrasing, and particular choices might create effects which are deemed especially effective."[17] This would appear to be an obvious case where imaginative thinking, i.e., thinking of possibilities, comes into play. The sense of imaginative thinking, as thinking of something as possibly being so, plays an important role in the art form of theatre, along with skill and technique.

> *If the notion of technique is limited to movement on stage, control of the voice and body, projection, and similar abilities, then the ability to act imaginatively and effectively must be viewed as something more. Yet surely the ability to understand a character and to create a believable presence on stage is a part of the actor's skill as well. Such a characterization comes not purely from a pre-existing abstract vision, but rather from the actor working with the script, director, and other actors and developing the characterization through technical abilities and acting skills. Once this is recognized, we can see here again that the notions of imagination and skill are not easily separated.*[18]

The idea of a "pre-existing abstract vision" implies that skills are not involved in imaginative thinking. However, as

Bailin points out, this does not appear to be the case when art is created. "It is not the case that the artist possesses a full-blown imaginative vision totally independent of the skills constitutive of the art. Rather, higher-order skills necessarily involve imagination and these skills contribute to and are an integral part of the development of the imaginative vision."[19] These higher-order skills "are not a matter simply of proficiency in certain techniques, but rather a very sophisticated mastery based on a repertoire of lower order skills. This involves the integration of lower order skills, and considerable judgment."[20] It is the involvement of judgment wherein lies the work of the imagination. In making a judgment, one is considering alternatives. This is an instance of thinking of possibilities. Thus, there is an intimate connection between imaginative thinking and creating original and valuable products.

Educational Implications

When we perceive creative dance as an activity producing original and valuable products, the implications for educational practice are quite different from those resulting from a "free expression" view. Activities encouraging imaginative thinking, as well as knowledge and skills, are required to create original and valuable products.

The knowledge to be taught would include the principles of the discipline of which the creative activity is a part. Bailin states that

> the knowledge which is crucial to creative achievement is much more than merely an acquaintance with a body of facts. It involves, as well, an in-depth understanding of the principles and procedures of the discipline in question, of the method whereby inquiry proceeds, of the standards according to which reasons are assessed, and of the over-all goals and deep questions which are at issue.[21]

With regard to creative dance, the knowledge to be taught would include an understanding of movement principles. As

I mentioned in chapter one, learning basic movement principles can result from studying movement analyses such as the one proposed by Laban. Regarding "over-all goals and deep questions," the class should discuss the issue of the aesthetic nature of creative dance. That is, students should be made aware of the aesthetic potential of creative dance. This would involve teaching aesthetic features and aesthetic theories. Even in the early grades, students should be attempting to create aesthetically valuable dance pieces. These will not be of the same calibre as those created in the later grades, but young students can acquire an understanding of form early on when they realize that a dance has a beginning, a middle and an end, and that static positions are a good way to indicate a beginning and an end. Teaching effort qualities such as fast/slow and heavy/light will give students the ability to add variety to their movements. Older students can gain experience with these effort qualities in more complex combinations.

Closely linked to knowledge of movement is skill in using this knowledge, and closely linked to higher-order skills is the utilization of imaginative thinking. As I mentioned earlier, proponents of the free-expression movement often view the learning of skills/knowledge as an obstacle to participation in imaginative activities. This is especially true in the area of creative dance. Too often, teachers of creative dance feel that spending time learning about movement principles or aesthetic features detracts from time spent in "free-expressive" movement. However, time spent acquiring knowledge and higher-order skills (those requiring imaginative thinking) is not only worthwhile, but necessary, if students are to create aesthetically valuable dance pieces. Bailin emphasizes this contention.

> ... *skill and knowledge are not inhibiting, but rather open the way for creative achievement. High order skills are not merely mechanized habits but involve critical judgment applied in a variety of changing circumstances. Thus the teaching of skills as flexible abilities related to ends which may vary might obviate the possibility of rigidity and mechanization.*[22]

The teaching of skills as flexible abilities is intimately connected with the conception of imaginative thinking as thinking of possibilities or as thinking of something as possibly being so. This connection between the imagination and skills might not sit well with the creative dance teacher who feels that he/she is fostering the imagination by asking students to move like bunnies. However, skills *are* involved in this imaginative activity. When children are asked to move like bunnies, they are asked to make a judgment regarding what kind of movement a bunny makes. They may think of a number of possibilities. They may think of moving on all fours or they might hop on two feet. They make this decision in conjunction with the use of a locomotor skill. Their skill level may place constraints on their possible movement choices, i.e., if they are unable to coordinate their hands and feet, they will not be able to choose the possibility of moving on all fours. The children may also utilize their skills of applying effort qualities, i.e., they might hop very fast or they might be the Easter Bunny hopping methodically from one hiding spot to another. Whether the children explore different possibilities or whether they decide on one right away, the children also have to think imaginatively in the sense of thinking of themselves as possibly being bunnies. Thus, the imagination is fostered, but this occurs in conjunction with the development of high order skills. It should be recognized that many of the seemingly simple activities done in the name of creative dance utilize high order skills.

Conclusions

The purpose of this book was to provide a justification for the inclusion of creative dance in the educational curriculum; to show why creative dance should be included in the educational curriculum and what creative dance education would have to look like in order to provide this sort of educational value. First, I suggested that creative dance is aesthetic in nature. I do not deny that creative dance has value as physical education, as therapy or as an integrative subject. However, some of its strongest features are aesthetic. For example, the movement elements which constitute the basis for creative dance lessons include aesthetic features such as the symmetrical use of the body, balance in regards to one dancer as well as between dancers on the stage, the flow of a movement, etc. Creative dance fits under the aesthetic theory of expressionism in that movement is typically used to express feelings and emotions. Aesthetic features such as those I mentioned earlier are utilized in this expression. Thus, we should view creative dance first and foremost as an art form.

Second, I suggested that aesthetic activity can be justified based on the rich understanding which it is possible to attain through aesthetic activity. Once again, I am not denying the intrinsic value of aesthetic activity. However, I suggest that the potential to foster understanding through creative dance is an extrinsic value whose strength should justify the inclusion of creative dance in the educational curriculum. The understanding gained from experiencing how the content of a work of art is expressed is unique, involving interpretive rather than inductive or deductive reasoning. Understanding gained from aesthetic activity is sensuous in nature. The "richness" is a result of the close connection between reason and feeling, which is fundamental to aesthetic experiences. Experiencing particular works of art evokes feelings which lead to a greater understanding of the human experience. Students can attain this rich understanding, paradigmatically, through aesthetic experience, thus providing a convincing justification for aesthetic activity.

It then follows that creative dance should be included in the educational curriculum. However, there are still the issues of creativity and imagination which I discussed in the consideration of creative dance as an aesthetic activity. In conceptualizing the imagination as thinking of possibilities or of something as possibly being so, I suggested that imaginative thinking was fundamental to interpretive reasoning, which was necessary for the attainment of understanding through the appreciation of works of art. I also made a connection between imaginative thinking and the employment of skills and knowledge, i.e., high order skills requiring judgment, which require the thinking of possibilities. These skills and knowledge are necessary if students are to create original and valuable products. If these products involve aesthetic features, then they are aesthetic in nature. Thus there follows a sequence of imaginative thinking being required for the appreciation and creation of aesthetically valuable products. However, this sequence is not truly linear. If aesthetic activity fosters understanding, then understanding is gained from this experience and this understanding can form the basis of further imaginative thinking, and the cycle begins again. Rather than use the cycle metaphor, it would be more appropriate to use a spiral metaphor. The more exposure students have to aesthetic activity, the greater the attainment of understanding, and there is an increase in their "data base" of thoughts and feelings, which increases their potential for imaginative thinking, which increases their potential to appreciate and create aesthetically valuable products, and the spiral continues upward. This spiraling increase of understanding would seem to be an important educational goal and one which should easily justify the inclusion of creative dance in the educational curriculum.

Notes

1 E. Wiseman, "Process – Not Product: Guidelines for Adding Creative Dance to the Elementary School Curriculum," *Journal of Physical Education and Recreation*, 50 (1979): 47.

2 S. Bailin, "Theatre, Drama Education and the Role of the Aesthetic," *Journal of Curriculum Studies*, 25 (Sept./Oct. 1993): 428.

3 R. Laban, *Modern Educational Dance*, 3rd edition (Boston: Play, Inc., 1975), pp. 25-51.

4 See, for example, V. Preston-Dunlop, *A Handbook for Dance in Education* (Estover, Plymouth: MacDonald & Evans Ltd., 1980); Joyce, *First Steps in Teaching Creative Dance to Children* (Palo Alto, CA: Mayfield Publishing Company, 1980); J. Boorman, *Creative Dance in the First Three Grades* (Don Mills, Ontario: Longmans Canada, 1969).

5 See, for example, the K-12 Physical Education Manitoba Curriculum Guide, 1981.

6 Laban, *Modern Educational Dance*, pp. 59-75.

7 G. Bantock, "The Arts in Education," in P. Abbs, ed., *The Symbolic Order: A Contemporary Reader on the Arts Debate* (London: Falmer Press, 1989), p. 54.

8 Abbs, *The Symbolic Order*, p. 9.

9 Ibid.

10 H. Gardner, *Art, Mind and Brain* (New York: Basic Books, 1982), p. 217.

11 K. Stockhausen, *Towards a Cosmic Music* (London: Element Books, 1989), p. 49.

12 R. Ritson, "Creative Dance: A Systematic Approach to Teaching Children," *Journal of Physical Education, Recreation and Dance* 57 (1986): 70.

13 A. Sheppard, *Aesthetics: An Introduction to the Philosophy of Art* (Oxford: Oxford University Press, 1987), p. 14.

14 Ibid., p. 23.

15 Ibid., p. 70.

16 S. Bailin, *Achieving Extraordinary Ends: An Essay on Creativity* (Dordrecht: Kluwer Academic Publishers, 1988), p. 109.

17 Ibid., p. 112.

18 Ibid., p. 116.

19 Ibid., pp. 114-115.

20 Ibid., p. 113.

21 Ibid., p. 130.

22 Ibid.

23 Abbs, *The Symbolic Order*, p. 1.

Bibliography

Abbs, P., ed. *The Symbolic Order: A Contemporary Reader on the Arts Debate*. London: Falmer Press, 1989.

Abbs, P. "Aesthetic Education: An Opening Manifesto." In *The Symbolic Order: A Contemporary Reader on the Arts Debate*, ed. P. Abbs. London: Falmer Press, 1989.

Abbs, P. "The Pattern of Art-Making." In *The Symbolic Order: A Contemporary Reader on the Arts Debate*, ed. P. Abbs. London: Falmer Press, 1989.

Abinun, J. "Creativity and Education: Some Critical Remarks." *The Journal of Aesthetic Education* 15 (1981): 17-29.

Alter, J. "A Manifesto for Creative Dance in the Schools: Arts and Bodies are Basic." *Design* 85 (July/Aug. 1984): 26-33.

Apel, K. "Perspectives for a General Hermeneutic Theory." In *The Hermeneutics Reader*, ed. K. Mueller-Vollmer. New York: Continuum Publishing Company, 1985.

Aristotle. *De Anima*, III 427a28 - 427b26.

Arnold, P. "Creativity, Self-Expression, and Dance." *Journal of Aesthetic Education* 20 (1986): 49-58.

Bailin, S. *Achieving Extraordinary Ends: An Essay on Creativity*. Dordrecht: Kluwer Academic Publishers, 1988.

Bailin, S. "Other People's Products: The Value of Performing and Appreciating." *The Journal of Aesthetic Education* 27 (Summer 1993): 59-69.

Bailin, S. "Theatre, Drama Education and the Role of the Aesthetic." *Journal of Curriculum Studies* 25 (Sept./Oct. 1993): 423-432.

Bantock, G. "The Arts in Education." In *The Symbolic Order: A Contemporary Reader on the Arts Debate*, ed. P. Abbs. London: Falmer Press, 1989.

Barrow, R. "Some Observations on the Concept of Imagination." In *Imagination and Education*, eds. K. Egan & D. Nadaner. New York: Teachers College Press, 1988.

Best, D. *Feeling and Reason in the Arts*. London: Allen & Unwin, 1985.

Best, D. *Philosophy and Human Movement*. London: George Allen & Unwin, 1978.

Best, D. *The Rationality of Feeling*. London: The Falmer Press, 1992.

Biology: The Study of Life. Allyn & Bacon, 1987. (High-School Biology Textbook).

Blackwell, C. "Providing Every Child Opportunity to Dance." *Journal of Physical Education and Recreation* 50 (Sept. 1979): 55.

Boorman, J. *Creative Dance in the First Three Grades*. Don Mills, Ontario: Longmans Canada, 1969.

Carr, D. "Dance Education, Skill, and Behavioral Objectives." *Journal of Aesthetic Education* 18 (1984): 67-76.

Casey, E. *Imagining: A Phenomenological Study*. Bloomington, Indiana: Indiana University Press, 1976.

Clark, W. "Some Thoughts on Teaching Creativity." *Journal of Aesthetic Education* 20 (1986): 27-31.

Collingwood, R. *The Principles of Art*. Oxford: The Claredon Press, 1938.

Crawford, D. "The Questions of Aesthetics." In *Aesthetics and Arts Education*, eds. R. Smith and A. Simpson. Urbana, Illinois: University of Illinois Press, 1991.

Crittenden, B. "Education and Creativity." In *Concepts in Education: Philosophical Studies*. Melbourne: A Mercy Teachers' College – 20th Century Publication, 1973.

Dimondstein, G. *Exploring the Arts with Children*. New York: MacMillan Publishing Co., 1974.

Dimondstein, G. "The Place of Dance in General Education." *Journal of Aesthetic Education* 19 (1985): 77-84.

Ducasse, C. "The Subjectivity of Aesthetic Value." In *Introductory Readings in Aesthetics*, ed. J. Hospers. New York: The Free Press, 1969.

Edry, A. "Dance for Non-Dancers." *Design* 85 (July/Aug. 1894): 34-38.

Egan, K. *Imagination in Teaching and Learning: The Middle School Years.* London, Ontario: The Althouse Press, 1992.

Feyerabend, P. *Against Method: Outline of an Anarchistic Theory of Knowledge.* Atlantic Highlands, N. J.: Humanities Press, 1975.

Fleming, G. *Creative Rhythmic Movement: Boys and Girls Dancing.* New Jersey: Prentice-Hall, Inc., 1976.

Gardner, H. *Art, Mind and Brain.* New York: Basic Books, 1982.

Greene, M. "Art Worlds in Schools." In *The Symbolic Order: A Contemporary Reader on the Arts Debate,* ed. P. Abbs. London: Falmer Press, 1989.

H'Doubler, M. *Dance: A Creative Art Experience.* Madison, Wisconsin: The University of Wisconsin Press, 1957.

Hirst, P. "Literature and the Fine Arts as a Unique Form of Knowledge." *Knowledge and the Curriculum: A Collection of Philosophical Papers.* London: Routledge & Kegan Paul, 1974.

Howard, R. *Three Faces of Hermeneutics.* Berkeley: University of California Press, 1982.

Howard, V. *Artistry: The Work of Artists.* Indianapolis: Hackett Publishing Company, 1982.

Hume, D. *A Treatise of Human Nature.* ed. L. A. Selby-Bigge, 2nd ed. London: Oxford University Press, 1978, first published 1888.

Joyce, M. *First Steps in Teaching Creative Dance to Children,* 2nd edition. Palo Alto, CA: Mayfield Publishing Company, 1980.

K-12 Physical Education Manitoba Curriculum Guide, 1981.

Kant, I. *Critique of Pure Reason.* trans. J. M. D. Meiklejohn. London: J. M. Dent & Sons, Ltd., 1984, first published 1781.

Kneller, G. *The Art and Science of Creativity.* New York: Holt, Rinehart and Winston, Inc., 1966.

Koestler, A. *The Act of Creation.* London: Pan Books Ltd., 1964.

Krohn, J. "The Dance Dilemma: Where Does it Fit – Physical Education or Arts Education?" *Canadian Association of Health, Physical Education and Recreation Journal* 57 (Fall 1991): 47-49.

Kuhn, T. *The Structure of Scientific Revolutions,* 2nd ed. Chicago: University of Chicago Press, 1970.

Laban, R. *Modern Educational Dance,* 3rd ed. Boston: Play, Inc., 1975.

Lockhart, A. & Pease, E. *Modern Dance: Building and Teaching Lessons,* 6th ed. Dubuque, Iowa: W. C. Brown Company Publishers, 1982.

MacDonald, C. "Creative Dance in Elementary Schools: A Theoretical and Practical Justification." *Canadian Journal of Education* 16 (1991): 434-441.

Macdonald, J. *A Philosophy of Education.* Toronto: W. J. Gage Ltd., 1965.

Maitland, J. "Creativity." *Journal of Aesthetics and Art Criticism* 34 (Summer 1976): 397-409.

Marcuse, H. *The Aesthetic Dimension.* Boston: Beacon Press, 1978.

Maritain, J. "Creative Intuition in Art and Poetry." In *The Creativity Question,* ed. A. Rothenberg and C. Hausman. Durham, N. C.: Duke University Press, 1976.

McColl, S. "Dance as Aesthetic Education." *Journal of Physical Education, Health and Recreation* 50 (Sept. 1979): 44-46.

Meynell, H. *The Nature of Aesthetic Value.* Albany: State University of New York Press, 1986.

Morawski, S. *Inquiries into the Fundamentals of Aesthetics.* Cambridge, Massachusetts: The MIT Press, 1974.

Morin, F. *Psychological and Curricular Foundations for Elementary Dance Education.* Edina, MN: Bellwether Press, 1988.

Mozart, W. "A Letter." In *Creativity,* ed. P. Vernon. New York: Penguin Books Ltd., 1970.

Murray, R. "A Statement of Belief." In *Children's Dance*, ed. G. Fleming. Washington, D.C.: AAHPER Publications, 1973.

Nussbaum, M. *Love's Knowledge: Essays on Philosophy and Literature.* Oxford: Oxford University Press, 1990.

Perkins, D. "Creativity by Design." *Educational Leadership* 42 (1984): 18-25.

Perkins, D. *The Mind's Best Work.* Cambridge: Harvard University Press, 1981.

Plato. *Ion*, 543b.

Plato. *The Republic*, Book X 597.

Preston-Dunlop, V. *A Handbook for Dance in Education.* Estover, Plymouth: MacDonald & Evans Ltd., 1980.

Rader, M. & Jessup, B. *Art and Human Value.* New Jersey: Prentice-Hall, Inc., 1976.

Redfern, H. "Aesthetic Understanding." In *Aesthetics and Arts Education*, eds. R. Smith and A. Simpson. Urbana, Illinois: University of Illinois Press, 1991.

Redfern, H. *Concepts in Modern Educational Dance.* London: Henry Kimpton Publishers, 1973.

Redfern, H. *Questions in Aesthetic Education.* London: Allen & Unwin Publishers, 1986.

Richmond, S. "Art and Politics in John Berger's Novel A Painter of Our Time." *Journal of Social Theory and Art Education* 11 (June 1991): 26-34.

Richmond, S. "Once Again: Art Education, Politics, and the Aesthetic Perspective." *Canadian Review of Art Education* 16 (1989): 119-128.

Richmond, S. "Three Assumptions that Influence Art Education: A Description and a Critique." *Journal of Aesthetic Education* 25 (1991): 1-15.

Ritson, R. "Creative Dance: A Systematic Approach to Teaching Children." *Journal of Physical Education, Recreation and Dance* 57 (1986): 67-78.

Rubin, L. "Teaching Creative Dance." *Design* 80 (Sept. 1979): 26-28.

Russell, B. *The Problems of Philosophy*. New York: Oxford University Press, 1959.

Ryle, G. *The Concept of Mind*. New York: Barnes & Noble, Inc., 1949.

Sartre, J. P. *Imagination: A Psychological Critique*, trans. Forrest William. Ann Arbor: The University of Michigan Press, 1962.

Sartre, J. P. *The Psychology of Imagination*, trans. Bernard Frechtman. New York: Washington Square Press, Inc., 1966.

Schul-Pfeffer, J. "Creative Dance/Movement as a Teaching Tool." *Design* 82 (Oct. 1980): 34-37.

Scruton, R. *Art and Imagination: A Study of the Philosophy of Mind*. London: Metheun & Co. Ltd., 1974.

Shapiro, L. "Dancing in the Schools." *Design* 79 (Sept. 1978): 8-12.

Sheppard, A. *Aesthetics: An Introduction to the Philosophy of Art*. Oxford: Oxford University Press, 1987.

Sparshott, F. "Contexts of Dance." *Journal of Aesthetic Education* 24 (Spring, 1990): 73-87.

Stanley, S. *Physical Education: A Movement Orientation*, 2nd ed. Toronto: McGraw-Hill Ryerson, 1977.

Stockhausen, K. *Towards a Cosmic Music*. London: Element Books, 1989.

Tchaikovsky, P. "Letters. " In *Creativity*, ed. P. Vernon. New York: Penguin Books Ltd., 1970.

Warnock, M. *Imagination*. London: Faber and Faber, 1976.

Weisberg, R. *Creativity: Genius and Other Myths*. New York: W. H. Freeman and Co., 1986.

Wells, L. "Children on the Move." *Design* 80 (Sept. 1979): 14-18.

White, A. *The Language of Imagination*. Oxford: Basil Blackwell, 1990.

White, J. "Creativity and Education: A Philosophical Analysis." *British Journal of Educational Studies* 16 (1969): 123-137.

Winchester, I. "Creation and Creativity in Art and Science." *Interchange* 16 (1985): 70-76.

Winchester, I. *Notes on Aesthetics.* Unpublished manuscript, February 10, 1978.

Wiseman, E. "Process – Not Product: Guidelines for Adding Creative Dance to the Elementary School Curriculum." *Journal of Physical Education and Recreation*, 50 (1979): 47-49.

Zirulnik, A. & Young, J. "Help Them 'Jump for Joy'." *Journal of Physical Education and Recreation* 50 (Sept. 1979): 43.